D1605729

TRANSFORMATIONAL
LEADERSHIP AND
HIGH-INTENSITY INTERVAL TRAINING

OTHER PUBLICATIONS BY CAROL R. HIMELHOCH

Himelhoch, C.R. (2012, September). Synergistic learning community: Bringing out the best in others in an on-line course. Invited Speaker at the Lilly Conference on College and University Teaching, Traverse City, MI.

Antonaros, M.E., Himelhoch, C.R., & Ball, S.R. (2011, April). Unpacking leader effectiveness: Exploring gender, institutional type, and other common predictors. Presented at the American Educational Research Association conference (AERA), New Orleans, LA.

Dey, E. L., Antonaros, M., & Himelhoch, C. R. (2007). Strangers in a strange land: Faculty leadership in context. Presented at the American Educational Research Association conference (AERA) Annual Meeting, Chicago, IL.

Dey, E.L., Ross, P., White, C.B., & Himelhoch, C.R. (2007). A different kind of diversity outcome: Medical school experiences associated with physician choices to serve the underserved. Presented at the American Educational Research Association conference (AERA) Annual Meeting, Chicago, IL.

MindBodyMed Press Mini-Monograph Series

TRANSFORMATIONAL LEADERSHIP AND HIGH-INTENSITY INTERVAL TRAINING

CAROL R. HIMELHOCH, PhD

University of Michigan-Educated

Professor of Management

MindBodyMed
Press

Spring Lake | Michigan | United States
Edited by Michele Spilberg Hart, MA

Publisher: MindBodyMed Press, LLC, PO Box 221
Spring Lake, Michigan, United States
www.MindBodyMedPress.com

Ordering Information:
Quantity sales. Special discounts are available on quantity purchases
by corporations, associations, book clubs, and others. For details,
contact the publisher at the address above.

Publisher's Cataloging-in-Publication data

Himelhoch, Carol Rose.
    Transformational leadership and high-intensity interval training /
Carol R. Himelhoch, PhD.
    p. cm.
    ISBN 9780990329718 (pbk.)
    ISBN 9780990329725 (e-book)
    Includes bibliographical references and index.

1. Leadership. 2. Executive ability. 3. Organizational effectiveness. 4.
Job stress. 5. Occupational health. 6. Endurance sports --Psychological
aspects. 7. Physical fitness --Psychological aspects. 8. Exercise --Psycho-
logical aspects. 9. Aerobic exercise. 10. Cardiovascular fitness. I. Title.

HD57.7 .H558 2014
658.4 --dc23   2014945063

Dedication

I dedicate this book to my parents, Charles and Isabel Himelhoch, and my brother, Chip Himelhoch, all of whom supported my passion for mind-body connections and fitness early and throughout my life.

Medical Disclaimer

Health care is an ever-changing field. MindBodyMed Press, its editors, and authors of the mini-monographs, monographs, and creative nonfiction books have made every effort to provide information that is accurate and complete as of the date of publication and consistent with standards of good practice in the health care setting. As research and practice advance, however, standards may change. For this reason it is recommended that readers evaluate the applicability of any recommendations in light of particular situations and changing standards.

MindBodyMed Press mini-monographs, monographs, and creative nonfiction books are designed for educational purposes only and MindBodyMed Press, its editors, and authors are not engaged in rendering medical advice or professional services. The information provided in this book should not be used for diagnosing or treating a health problem or a disease. It is not a substitute for professional care. Members of the public using this book are advised to consult with a physician regarding personal medical care. If you have or suspect you may have a health problem, consult your health care provider.

Although the author and publisher have made every effort to ensure that the information in this book was correct at press time, the author and publisher do not assume and hereby disclaim any liability to any party for any loss, damage, or disruption caused by errors or omissions, whether such errors or omissions result from negligence, accident, or any other cause.

Always consult your primary health care provider before beginning any exercise program.

Table of Contents

List of Figures

List of Tables

Publisher's Welcome

While working on developing *MindBodyMed Press*, it became clear that *MindBodyMed Press* was going to become an indie publisher that would fill a void that exists in the way scientific information is shared with the public. The Internet has given everyone a voice as blogging platforms opened the door for anyone to spew words in digital format, making immediately available for public consumption any information, whether it is based on sound principles or mere ill-conceived opinions of self-appointed experts.

The National Center for Complementary and Alternative Medicine (NCCAM) draws attention to the problem in its Third Strategic Plan (2011-2015) in which the agency states that

> *Although a vast amount of information about CAM [Complementary and Alternative Medicine] is available in the public domain, much of it is incomplete, misleading, inaccurate, or based on scientifically unproven claims. Much of the public's use of CAM occurs in the absence of advice or guidance from health care providers (conventional or CAM)* (p. 14).

On the other extreme of the spectrum are peer-reviewed journals that serve the scientific community only.

Many of these traditional journals hide information behind well-gated databases, accessible only with costly annual subscriptions or per-paper charges that lie outside the pocketbooks of the average reader. One such example is a publisher who lists individual articles of a journal at a pay-per-view charge (access for 24 hours) at US $51 and unlimited access to said journal at an annual subscription of $1,038. The average per-article purchase price of another well-respected full-text scientific database is $35.95. **MindBodyMed Press's** titles are available for $7.99 and upwards in trade paperback and $6.99 and upwards in eBook format.

Falling in the middle are open-access peer review journals, which are free to consumers yet have a whole set of problems on their own, accepting bogus scientific research, seemingly more concerned with collecting hefty up-front charges from authors rather than helping the scientific community through peer review. For a thorough report on the state of affairs in the open-access scientific enterprise read "Who's Afraid of Peer Review?" by John Bohannon (2013). According to Bohannon, scientists agree that the open-access model itself is not to blame. One scientist describes the situation as not too much different than traditional subscription-based journals.

Despite this, the direction **MindBodyMed Press** is taking is no replacement for a thorough peer review in a reputable scientific journal. Scientific peer review, along with the cumbersome collection, interpretation, and reporting of data is necessary to inform health care providers, payers, employers, and patients of scientific data, allowing better evidence-based decision making pertaining to the use of mind-body interventions, practices, and disciplines.

However, peer review is usually a lengthy process and sometimes can take years.

Up until now, there has been no happy medium to afford the public access to the scientific literature. It simply is too expensive! Though things seem to be changing. The other day, while skimming The Chronicle of Higher Education, I came across an interesting article titled "The Rise of the Mini-Monograph" written by Leonardo Cassuto (2013).

A monograph, according to Merriam-Webster is "...a learned treatise on a small area of learning ... a written account of a single thing" (Merriam-Webster Dictionary, n.d.). Up until recently, a monograph was considered a one-volume work giving in depth treatment to a specialized subject, written by a scholar in the field, for mainly an academic audience (University of Illinois at Urbana-Champaign, n.d.).

According to Cassuto's (2013) article, however, several academic departments and scholarly presses are experimenting with shorter formats. Enter the mini-monograph. An entirely new book format, so to speak. The definitions from the previous paragraph still apply, though the length of the work is slightly smaller. Presses have begun using this new category to acquire and market original work. *MindBodyMed Press* is one of those presses.

Publisher Palgrave Pivot aims to attract original works between 30,000 and 50,000 words in length. Stanford Briefs publishes mini-monographs in the 20,000 to 40,000-word range. We at *MindBodyMed Press* believe that original works between 4,000 and 50,000 words, with

20,000-40,000 words being ideal, have considerable potential to reach a broad audience.

Like our counterpart Stanford Briefs, *MindBodyMed Press* believes that the purpose of making mini-monographs available to a wider audience is to foster "…an open argument rather than adding to a long conversation" (Cassuto, 2013). However, unlike Palgrave Pivot and Stanford Briefs, *MindBodyMed Press's* future lies in the integrative medicine niche market. According to NCCAM, practitioners integrating complementary and alternative medicine (CAM) for which there is some scientific evidence of safety and effectiveness into mainstream medicine are the key holders of knowledge related to the possible use of CAM in main stream medicine. These practitioners are in a good position to provide and share information that is of value to the public and health care providers (National Center for Complementary and Alternative Medicine, 2011).

What type of author should consider publishing with MindBodyMed Press and why?

MindBodyMed Press is a platform that allows practitioners embracing integrative medicine, be that medical doctors, nurses, nutritionists, CAM & mind- body medicine practitioners, and research scientists to connect with the public in a new format – the mini-monograph.

MindBodyMed Press closes the gap in the current publication process by changing the way integrative medicine practitioners communicate with the public, exposing their titles on mainstream platforms such as trade paperback and eBook (enhanced ePub v.3) publication through popular platforms such as Amazon.com, Kindle, Kobo, iBooks, etc. rather than specialized databases.

MindBodyMed Press aims for a quick turnaround: Less than three months from acceptance to publication in most cases.

Especially appealing to authors is that unlike traditional peer review publishing, the author retains copyright to their work. The author also receives royalties from the sale of their work. Yes! Unlike traditional peer review publishing, anytime an author's work is sold, he/she will receive royalties.

Publication with *MindBodyMed Press* is ideal for CAM and mind-body scientists, clinicians, and practitioners integrating those practices into mainstream medicine that do not want or do not need to subject themselves to a lengthy peer review process.

On the other hand, *MindBodyMed Press* also aims to be an indie publishing company for graduate students and junior faculty. According to Cassuto's article, Stephen Greenblatt, an American literary critic, theorist, and scholar at Harvard University, warned a decade ago not to force "…the most vulnerable members of the academic community - that is graduate students and junior faculty members - to fulfill outmoded requirements" (Cassuto, 2013). Cassuto continues to write that the best way to marshal in new practices is to support them.

At *MindBodyMed Press* we work closely with nonfiction authors, be that seasoned pros, or up and coming experts in the field of integrative medicine to create and share high quality information. In order for a manuscript to be considered for publication, authors must follow accepted scientific processes for original research (quantitative, qualitative, mixed methods research, reporting of case studies, and literature reviews) and/or best practices for nonfiction literary titles.

So, *MindBodyMed Press* will be adding quality CAM and mind-body medicine information from medical doctors, nurses, nutritionists, and research scientists to mainstream medicine. This information would have otherwise withered away on a researcher's or clinician's computer hard drive, never to see the light of day again, because it was either too long for peer review, and too short for a full length book.

Who do we serve?

MindBodyMed Press serves consumers who are curious about what the science says, as well as individuals with strong, often polar-opposite beliefs or biases regarding the state of evidence about CAM and mind-body interventions—or even the need for mind-body research.

MindBodyMed Press will present innovative new books, called mini-monographs, published to address the quintessence of a CAM or mind-body medicine modality. Mini-monographs are selected based on basic scientific criteria without sacrificing the quality of carefully edited and produced content. Mini-monographs will be published quickly promoting mindful, intelligent debate, while bringing novel perspectives and theoretical approaches within the reach of experts as well as the public.

MindBodyMed Press believes that you have a right to know what practitioners integrating CAM or mind-body modalities into mainstream medicine are doing right now to help people with their chronic ailments. If you are a cancer patient, you might not have years to wait for this process to play out in peer review. You need high quality information immediately in order to discern with your health care team if a CAM or mind-body modality might be beneficial in your particular case.

The only way this can happen is if you have access to timely information from the providers on the health care front, even if this information does not yet lead to conclusive evidence. Adhering to this publication model will allow *MindBodyMed Press* to put high quality integrative medical knowledge within economical reach of the public.

I am happy to share *MindBodyMed Press's* mission and vision with you here.

MindBodyMed Press's Vision:

Utilizing 21st century science and information technology, we will empower CAM practitioners, mind-body practitioners, clinicians, and scientists, who are the key holders of knowledge related to the potential use of mind-body interventions, to provide and share information that is of value to the public and to health care providers.

MindBodyMed Press's Mission:

Given the reality of widespread and frequent self-care use of CAM and mind-body medicine,

> *MindBodyMed Press will strive to share CAM and mind-body medical information primarily to health care consumers and health care providers who are curious about CAM and mind-body medicine, even when the evidence is inconclusive or does not lead to clear guidance.*

If you are a CAM or mind-body-oriented health care provider such as medical doctor, nurse, social worker, psychologist, research scientist, graduate student, nutritionist, etc., please consider submitting your finished manuscript to *MindBodyMed Press*. We especially want to hear from you if you have a manuscript pertaining integrating CAM, a mind-body modality, or a nutritional intervention pertaining to cancer. The only caveat; we will review your manuscript and make sure it adheres to accepted guidelines within the area of research in which your manuscript falls (quantitative research, qualitative research, mixed methods research, literature reviews, case studies, nonfiction, and so forth).

If you are a consumer in a bookstore skimming through this book, thank you for browsing, and I hope that the information contained meets your standards and you will consider purchasing this title. Purchasing a title not only provides you with solid information but a purchase also supports up-and-coming scholars (in many cases) in CAM, as well as practitioners and or researchers who have taken the time to share their experiences derived from many patient encounters or original research.

In return, we hope that if you are a consumer looking to address a health problem that the information contained herein will start a healthy dialogue between you, your primary health care provider(s), and your loved ones that takes into account your personal preferences.

Please do not hesitate to contact me should you have any further questions about your manuscript or the publishing process with *MindBodyMed Press*. If you are a health care consumer who has feedback on how to make *MindBodyMed Press* more appealing to you, I welcome your feedback as well.

Welcome to *MindBodyMed Press*. Your Mind. Your Body. Unite Them.

Werner Absenger
Managing Editor and Publisher MindBodyMed Press
werner@MindBodyMedPress.com

References:

Bohannon, J. (2013). Who's afraid of peer review? Science, 342(6154), 60–65. doi:10.1126/science.342.6154.60

Cassuto, L. (2013, August 12). The rise of the mini-monograph. *The Chronicle of Higher Education.* Retrieved from https://chronicle.com/article/The-Rise-of-the-Mini-Monograph/141007/

Identifying a scholarly monograph. (n.d.). Retrieved from University of Illinois at Urbana-Champaign website: http://www.library.illinois.edu/learn/research/monograph.html

Monograph. (n.d.). In *Merriam-Webster's online dictionary.* Retrieved from http://www.merriamwebster.com/dictionary/monograph

National Center for Complementary and Alternative Medicine. (2011). *NCCAM's Third Strategic Plan: Exploring the science of complementary and alternative medicine* (Third Strategic Plan). Retrieved from http://nccam.nih.gov/sites/nccam.nih.gov/files/NCCAM_SP_508.pdf

Acknowledgements

I would like to offer my special thanks to my friend and colleague, Dr. Jim Sam, for reviewing my manuscript. My great appreciation also is extended to writer and poet Cindy Frenkel, who made the time to apply her editorial genius to the first chapter. I attempted to use principles I learned from her to the remainder.

I extend a heartfelt thanks to Dr. Aaron Anderson, Director of Strategic Organizational Initiatives at San Francisco State University, who helped me strategize the final format for this monograph. I am especially grateful to Dr. Allan Afuah, Associate Professor of Strategy at the Stephen M. Ross School of Business at The University of Michigan, and Miki Carey, head coach and owner of Gardens Cross-Fit in Palm Beach Gardens, Florida, both of whom were willing to endorse my work.

This study was made possible by the participants I interviewed, and toward them I feel deep gratitude. Confidentiality agreements preclude me from naming them, however they were extremely generous with their time and assistance.

Kathy Blough, my good friend, put me in touch with Werner Absenger of MindBodyMed Press, the perfect outlet for disseminating my work. Thank you, Kathy. Thank you, Werner. Rukmini Vasupuram, Esq., my dear friend, you offered your essential perspective, expertise, and support at short notice when I needed help. Thank you.

Finally, I wish to thank my husband, Dr. Stephen Ball. Thank you, Steve, for taking my photo for the cover. Steve tried in earnest to distance himself from this project but was roped in regardless. He remains clueless in grasping the enormity of his contribution.

Carol R. Himelhoch
Ann Arbor, Michigan
March, 2014

MindBodyMed Press Mini-Monograph Series

TRANSFORMATIONAL LEADERSHIP AND HIGH-INTENSITY INTERVAL TRAINING

CAROL R. HIMELHOCH, PHD

University of Michigan-Educated

Professor of Management

MindBodyMed
Press

Spring Lake | Michigan | United States
Edited by Michele Spilberg Hart, MA

[1]

ABSTRACT

Transformational leadership has been tested empirically more than other models, and scholars consider it well-suited to high-stress business climates.

No studies have examined comprehensively the leader's level of physical fitness as an antecedent to transformational leadership. In this exploratory study, the ways in which the lived experiences of avid exercisers intersect with their leadership styles were examined. The results suggest mind-body connections in which physically-fit leaders are apt to perceive transformational approaches to their leadership.

Keywords: transformational leadership,
                occupational stress,
                psychological well-being,
                mind-body health,
                physical fitness,
                complementary medicine,
                high-intensity interval training

1

A new way to think about fitness, health, and occupation.

– Miki Carey, Owner, Gardens CrossFit, a
"Top 15 CrossFit Gyms in America," per Spotmegirl.com

Miki Carey, owner of Gardens CrossFit, Palm Beach Gardens, Florida, performing a clean, which is one of many Olympic lifts in high-intensity exercise routines.

Photo Credit: Chris Walters, Coral Springs, Florida

[2]

INTRODUCTION

> *The healthy man does not torture others - generally it is the tortured who turns into torturers.*
>
> — Carl Jung (1875-1961)

Imagine walking into a gym, 200 pounds overweight, and working out for the first time in a class with elite athletes who are climbing ropes, jumping on tall boxes, and lifting barbells loaded with plates that are multiples of their own body weight. As a beginner, struggling to even finish the routine at all, let alone to complete it within a specified time, is overwhelming. Granted, the weights and number of repetitions may be scaled to match the fitness level of the individual athlete, however, such a setting would intimidate many. Imagine also finishing last, but receiving resounding cheers from everyone in class because they understand both the enormous challenge and accomplishment.

Such is an emblematic experience of many athletes who walk into a CrossFit® gym for the first time. Although they may not be 200 pounds overweight, they may relate with Juliet, a female scientist who walked into a high-intensity exercise class almost 10 years ago in a state of ill health. Her doctor warned her that she needed to change her lifestyle and lose weight or she would die. "I was a heart attack waiting to happen, and I could have died any minute." As a scientist and manager of pharmaceutical researchers, she realized "you can just be gone like that and now your passion is gone because you're gone." The only way that she could achieve her vision of "helping mankind" through the discovery of treatments for cancer, AIDS, pandemic flu, anthrax infections, and other diseases, was to work through the people she leads. She lost 200 pounds, eats well, and is alive and thriving as a scientist and mother.

Background, Problem, and Purpose

Obesity and related health problems afflict the American population. According to Jacob Seidell's (2014) chapter in the Handbook of Obesity: Epidemiology, Etiology, and Physiopathology, "…over 74% of American men and 65% of American women are now overweight or obese" (p. 48). Years ago, children played actively outside, ate minimally-processed foods, and sat passively in front of a television for limited periods. The shift to a sedentary life in which people spend hours on electronic devices, consuming processed and sugar-laden foods and beverages, is a growing concern. The problem is so widespread that First Lady Michelle Obama made reducing the obesity of American children her key agenda. Children advance to adulthood quickly and, when they populate organizations and management positions, many are in a state of poor health. Employers are beginning to pay attention to obesity rates because the costs associated with their health care affect their bottom lines (Luckhaupt, Cohen, Li, & Calvert, 2014).

The long-running battle with obesity has raised public awareness of the importance of diet and exercise. The physical benefits of weight loss have been examined extensively, and include a reduced risk of diseases such as cancer and diabetes, as well as a reduction in blood lipids and blood pressure (Colditz & Bohlke, 2014; Seimon et al., 2014), all of which are associated with many serious health consequences if not managed. An emerging research agenda is tackling the psychological benefits of weight loss. One exploratory meta-analysis of 36 studies found that weight reduction is associated with a decrease in depression as well as improved self-esteem, body image, and quality of life (Lasikiewicz, Myrissa, Hoyland, & Lawton, 2014). Privitera, Antonelli, and Szal (2014) found that physical exercise increases perceptions of a pleasant mood by 95%. In a study of Type D distressed personalities, Galit Amon (2014) exposed a correlation between the integration of physical activity into one's life and reduced burnout and heightened engagement.

There are two ways to address obesity. One is through diet; the other is through exercise (Church, 2014; Makris, Lent, & Foster, 2014; Westerteterp-Plantenga, 2014). My study focused on exercise, specifically to see how it relates to the mind of those occupying organizational leadership positions. Conditions in today's competitive markets put leaders under pressure to innovate rapidly, control costs, respond quickly to customers, manage complex supply chains, and continuously improve processes and quality (Mitra, 2014). Research in exercise science reveals the benefits of cardiovascular health and, more specifically, how regular exercise reduces stress, and helps people to cope with burnout, depression, and other stress-related emotional states (Jonsdottir, Gerber, Lindwall, Lindegard, & Borjession, 2014). Studies reveal that leaders who employ transformational leadership styles are better able to cope with changing business climates (Nanjundeswaras and Swamy, 2014). These studies have not yet determined if physically fit leaders transform both their bodies and their organizations because research connecting these two investigative domains is sparse.

Transformational leadership was introduced by Burns (1978) and Bass (1985), and has since been used in empirical investigations more than any other leadership theory (Barling, Christie, & Hoption, 2010; Barling, et al., 2012; Bono & Judge, 2004; Pflanz & Ogle, 2006). Four behaviors comprise transformational leadership: (1) idealized influence, in which the leader sets a good example and makes sacrifices to help employees; (2) intellectual stimulation, which entails rousing creativity in followers; (3) individualized consideration, a term for coaching, encouraging, and supporting followers; and (4) inspirational motivation, or instilling a motivating vision in followers (Yukl, 2013).

Most studies have examined the effects of transformational leader behavior on organizational dimensions such as subordinate self-efficacy, intentions to leave, and extra-role behaviors (Callier, 2014). The consequences are vital to understand, however, precursors of transformational leadership have received far less attention. Antecedents examined previously include the leader's personality, gender, intelligence, and self-confidence (Walter & Bruch, 2009). The problem, however, is that no studies have focused on the role of mind-body connections and their relationships to transformational leadership (Atwater & Yammarino, 1993; Gerdes, 2001; Neck & Cooper, 2000). The research presented herein attempts to start to address this gap. The purpose of this qualitative phenomenological study is to understand the way in which physical fitness connects to transformational leadership behaviors.

Review of the Relevant Literature

Mind-Body Connections

The premise of a mind-body connection has received empirical attention spanning a range of domains that include cancer treatments, emotional health, pain management, and psychoimmunology (Littrell, 2008; Pally, 1998; Sarno, 1991; Verhœf & White, 2002). The complementary medicine field is relatively new in the context of modern medicine, with more researchers attempting to explore the connection scientifically. The University of Minnesota's Center for Spirituality and Healing relies on James Gordon's definition of the mind-body connection: "The brain and peripheral nervous system, the endocrine and immune systems, and indeed, all the organs of our body and all the emotional responses we have, share a common chemical language and are constantly communicating with one another" (Meadows, September 2013, para 8). One aspect of the mind-body connection is the benefits of physical fitness that is brought about through exercise.

Neurological researchers from Vrije Universiteit Medical Center in Amsterdam (Douw, Niebœr, van Dijk, Stam, & Twisk, 2014) advocate the benefits of physical fitness, which include improved cognition. They measured VO_2

max, a gauge of aerobic capacity, and its association with brain-wave topology. They confirmed an association between physical fitness and intelligence. In the realm of connecting physical fitness to leadership, Woo, Chernyshenko, Stark, and Conz (2014) conducted a meta-analysis, and found a valid relation between the leader's intellect and organizational outcomes. Viewing the mind as part of the body, some scholars also have begun to explore how physical fitness helps individuals cope with organizational work stress.

Lovelace, Manz, and Alves (2007) developed a set of propositions concerning the role of physical fitness for the manager's "self leadership," a term defined as delegating and empowering employees to reduce the leader's burden. Their appraisal supports an association between high stress and a variety of diseases and cardiovascular conditions as well as other deleterious effects of psychological strain on psychological health. Their research shows that when physical fitness is a component of a leader's lifestyle the leader's engagement and regeneration levels increase.

Their propositions were based on a literature review and were not tested empirically. Çelik (2014) asserts that self leadership supports respecting each employee holistically. The assertion holds appeal, yet it has not been examined through rigorous research. Integrating the transformational leadership concept and physiological health into management is perhaps the most promising framework for modeling how to effectively lead employees for the mutual benefit of organizations and their members.

Transformational Leadership

Nanjundeswaras and Swamy (2014) argue that today's complex global environment relies on effective leaders who can readily adapt to this fast-paced, ever-changing world. According to Yukl (2013), most studies that concern transformational leadership emanated from James Burns's (1978) early work on political leadership. Therein Burns contrasted transactional and transformational leadership to isolate the transformational construct, which was new at the time.

Initially envisioned as fitting for highly-charged political environments, Burns considered transformational leadership a tool to raise the consciousness and ethical awareness of followers to bring about reform and change. By contrast, Burns argued that with transactional leadership, motivation emanates from a quid-pro-quo exchange that spurs action by appealing to the followers' self-interest. Values are present in transactional leadership, however, they are connected directly to perceived fairness and reciprocity in the exchanges. Transactional leadership relies on contingent rewards and punishment as well as management-by-exception (Burns, 1978; Yukl, 2013).

Since Burns's early work (1978), the conceptualization of transformational leadership has broadened from the political realm to achieving practical outcomes accomplished by tapping into the values and emotions of followers. The more current research draws mostly on the 1985 and 1996 studies conducted by Bass (Warrick, 2011; Yukl, 2013). In the updated theory (Bass, 1985, 1996; Yukl, 2013), followers of transformational leaders trust, admire, and respect their leaders; employees are more loyal and apt to exhibit organizational citizenship behaviors. The leader caters to employees' higher-order needs. In addition, employees understand the importance of the organization's goals and objectives, remaining open to putting their organization's or team's goals above their own. Transformational leaders exhibit the four behaviors mentioned previously: idealized influence, intellectual stimulation, individual consideration, and inspirational motivation (Yukl, 2013).

Antecedents to Transformational Leadership

Walter and Bruch (2009) extensively examined studies concerning the antecedents of transformational leadership, noting the relevance of the leader's traits and personalities. However, the studies often did not delineate a clean difference between transformational and charismatic leadership theories (Walter & Bruch, 2009; Yukl, 2013); more often than not they addressed charismatic leadership. Walter and Bruch's (2009) meta-analysis did support slight correlations between gender, intelligence, achievement-orientation, risk-taking propensity, self-confidence, trusting employees, and personal sensitivity as antecedents. Attwater and Yammarino (1993) looked at several attributes as antecedents, including physical fitness, intelligence, warmth, conformity, sensing/intuition, thinking/feeling, and emotional and behavioral coping. They found that these personal attributes explained 28% of the variance in transformational leadership behavior, however, they did not explore the physical fitness dimension comprehensively.

Barling and colleagues (2012) expanded the research on antecedents, incorporating the antecedent leader's psychological well-being. Specifically, they connected the absence of anxiety and/or distress of leaders on their behaviors. Although a mind-body connection is implied, the absence of distress as a definition of well-being is incomplete. Beyond the context of leadership or mind-body medicine research, well-being is defined in more positive terms. Robertson and Cooper (2010) derived a two-part definition of psychological well-being from their literature review. The first definition, *hedonic,* encompasses the experience of positive emotions or feeling good. The second definition, *eudaimonic*, is well-being experienced from achieving meaningful goals. Positive psychology researchers have shaped a similar two-part definition of psychological well-being that also considers positive emotions and a sense of purpose, and they build on each other in an upward spiral (Frederickson, 1998; Frederickson & Joiner, 2002; Robertson & Cooper, 2010; Seligman, Steen, Park, & Peterson, 2005). However, the studies do not address the physical fitness dimension or transformational leadership specifically.

Juniper (2011) offered a definition of well-being that includes physical health among a collection of well-being dimensions. Neck and Cooper (2000) suggested that physically fit executives are able to handle the demands and stress of their jobs better than those of lower fitness levels, yet they made no connection to the leader's well-being and the presence of a transformational leadership style. Gerdes (2001) posited a link between one's moral character, physical fitness, emotional intelligence, and leadership, but provided no empirical research to validate this connection.

Schippers and Hogenes (2011), Cross, Baker, and Parker (2003) identified people in organizations either as *energizers* or *de-energizers*, and found that energizers are higher performers. Schippers and Hogenes (2011) suggested that energetic employees attain goals sooner, have clear goals, achieve person-environment fit (a theoretical reference to values shared both by employees and the organization), and exhibit initiative and well-being. Hogenes offered also that transformational leaders may energize their subordinates more effectively than transactional leaders. The physical-fitness dimension was not addressed explicitly nor tested empirically in the study, although a connection between physical fitness and the leader's energy was implied.

Heaphy and Dutton (2008) contended "positive social interactions at work have beneficial physiological effects" (p. 137), and mentioned the need to regard leaders and employees more holistically. The mind-body connection was also suggested by Boyzatis, Smith, and Blase (2006), who made the case that leaders helping subordinates through coaching behaviors "experience psychophysiological effects that restore the body's natural healing and growth processes, thus enhancing their sustainability" (p. 8). Yet, neither study examined the connection between physical fitness and transformational leadership overtly.

Research has not explored the relationship between physical fitness and the extent to which individual managers adopt a transformational leadership style. A qualitative, exploratory study could support in part the launch of a research trajectory to better understand the mind-body relationship in connection with transformational leadership, a style of behavior considered well-suited to the current business climate.

[3]

METHODS

Research Question

The central research question that guided this qualitative phenomenological study is: *How do the lived experiences of avid exercisers intersect with their behavior as leaders?* Conceptually, avid exercise in this study refers to any form of high-intensity exercise working up to 80-90% of one's maximum heart rate, a level at which the athlete is breathless and able only to speak a few words for a sustained period. (Walking for 40 minutes is an example of lower intensity exercise.) The avid exerciser works out three or more times per week. The exploratory research design of this project delimits the focus on high-intensity exercise only. Sub-questions probed the extent to which physically-fit leaders exhibit transformational leadership behavior. In addition, the study questioned the ways in which physical fitness preceded their leadership behavior, the ways in which avid exercise changed them, and the connections between how they exercise and how they lead.

Method

Methods entailed interpretive phenomenological analysis with a modified Delphi technique to focus on the lived experiences of a population of physically-fit leaders who participate in high-intensity interval training (HIIT) on a regular basis.[1] According to Walter R. Thompson, Professor of Kinesiology and Health at Georgia State University, HIIT "Typically involves short bursts of high-intensity bouts of exercise followed by short periods of rest and recovery; these exercise programs usually take less than 30 minutes to perform" (Thompson, 2013, para.10). Examples of HIIT regimens include CrossFit®, Insanity®, and P90X®. The exercise routines are varied, and often emphasize functional movements that recruit the entire body versus isolating specific muscles or muscle groups. In CrossFit®, practitioners use the term "Workout of the Day" (WOD) in reference to these varied regimens. According to Martin Gibala, Professor of Kinesiology at McMaster University, HIIT can provide comparable or even superior physiological benefits compared to endurance training, yet the exercise procedures do not demand an enormous time commitment (Gibala, Little, MacDonald, & Hawley, 2012). Although other forms of exercise lead to fitness, HIIT was selected

Insanity® is a registered trademark of BEACHBODY, LLC. "Transformational Leadership and High-Intensity Interval Training" is an independent publication and is not affiliated with, nor has it been authorized, sponsored, or otherwise approved by BEACHBODY, LLC.

P90X® is a registered trademark of BEACHBODY, LLC. "Transformational Leadershipand High-Intensity Interval Training" is an independent publication and is not affiliated with, nor has it been authorized, sponsored, or otherwise approved by BEACHBODY, LLC.

in this exploratory study to set boundaries for a clean, operational definition of the practitioner's level of physical fitness. In the concluding chapter, I mention expanding the sample to include many and varied forms of exercise as a next research step; however, using only one form of exercise associated with physical fitness helped establish manageable boundaries for initial research. CrossFit® HIIT was useful in particular because this HIIT system has a benchmark workout, called Fight Gone Bad®, which is used in affiliate gyms worldwide to measure the fitness level of athletes. For the remainder of this book, "The Workout" will be used in reference to Fight Gone Bad®. References to workouts that are not surrounded by quotations pertain to non-benchmark exercise routines. The higher "The Workout" score, the more fit the athlete.

I interviewed five participants, which is toward the high end of the optimal non-probability sample size of three-to-six used in interpretive phenomenological analysis (Smith, Flowers, & Larkin, 2009). Although Smith et al. (2009) acknowledge a pressure for qualitative researchers to use a larger sample size, they note that interpretive phenomenological studies "benefit from a concentrated focus on a small number of cases" (p. 51), and specify the range of three-to-six participants as optimal. The sample size is large enough to explore themes and patterns, and minimizes the potential influence of bias of one participant. The first round of data was analyzed for common themes then circulated back to participants, who were asked to offer their critique and reflections. To qualify for selection in the study, the leaders must supervise at least seven employees, have participated at least three times per week in

Fight Gone Bad® is a registered trademark of CROSSFIT, INC. "Transformational Leadership and High-Intensity Interval Training" is an independent publication, and is not affiliated with, does not endorse, nor has it been authorized, sponsored, or otherwise approved by CROSSFIT, INC.

a HIIT class for more than one year, and have earned a score in "The Workout" greater than 250, which is a reflection of physical fitness. Both HIIT and "The Workout" were selected to isolate the construct of avid exercisers.

Phenomenological studies focus on the fundamental nature of human experience as perceived by participants (Creswell, 2009). Interpretive phenomenological analysis probes in-depth the lived experiences of participants who express their understanding in "their own terms" (Smith et al., 2009, p. 32) without forcing their analysis into pre-existing categories (Smith et al., 2009). According to Halling (2008), phenomenological research assumes participants are capable of providing reliable and complete descriptions and interpretations of their experiences, which leads to common conceptions across their lived experiences of the phenomena. This method is designed to elicit substantive and thoughtful data that shape the story of the participants' experiences, orientation, and approaches to understanding (Smith et al., 2009).

The modified Delphi technique benefits the research design because the lived experiences and opinions of participants go through an iterative and collaborative involvement of experts. Participants reviewed the findings, and reached consensus on the meaning derived from the data (Du Plessis & Human, 2007; Iqbal & Pipon-Young, 2009). The Delphi method is helpful when the sample population is geographically dispersed (Colton & Covert, 2007) and when only partial understanding of the phenomenon has been established (Skulmoski, Hartman, & Krahn, 2007).

The interview protocol asked a group of questions concerning how participants became involved in HIIT, how

HIIT changed them, and how they perceive their identity as HIIT athletes. A second set of questions probed how they experience their HIIT workouts, including their approach to and experiences with the demanding physical activity as well as their interactions with the other athletes. A third set of questions addressed leadership styles; these inquiries probed both transformational and transactional behaviors to tease out any contrast, if present. The final set of questions queried connections they perceive in their lives as high-intensity athletes and their approaches to leadership. Appendix A contains the interview protocol.

Sample

Phenomenological research uses purposive sampling to identify the fundamental nature of people's experiences as applied to an explicit phenomenon (Creswell, 2009). Interpretive phenomenological analysis focuses on how the phenomenon appears in the consciousness of participants (Lewis & Staehler, 2010) as opposed to how it appears to observers. The modified Delphi technique explored the judgments and knowledge of expert practitioners who are active participants in the phenomenon. According to Baker, Lovell, and Harris (2006), when the literature does not offer guidelines for participant selection criteria, "it becomes the responsibility of each researcher to choose the most appropriate group of experts and defend that choice" (p. 67). In addition, purposive sampling is useful in qualitative studies, when probing for insights related to an experience is necessary (Smith et al., 2009). Smith et al. (2009) point out that to offer insights into the experience, participant characteristics must be theoretically in alignment with the phenomenological prototype from the targeted subgroup.

Limitations of purposive sampling were considered before deciding to proceed. Colton and Covert (2007) note its appropriateness when the experiences of experts inform the analysis, but warn of the possibility of multiple entries and self-selection bias within groups. The research design overcomes these limitations because each participant had an equal opportunity to participate in the study, and each participant was limited by the same circumstances of availability and motivation to partake. Participants were recruited through a variety of avenues, including the message board used by the population of HIIT athletes in this study, individual gym owners, and individual HIIT athletes. From that set, five participants were selected. The five subjects signed an informed-consent agreement to ensure their anonymity. Their characteristics are provided in the table below. To help the reader form a mental picture of each participant's persona, the fictional names in Table 1 are used throughout the chapters reporting results.

Table 1. Participant Demographics

Age	Gender	Fictional Name	Profession/ Industry
40	Male	Greg	President of a Warehouse and Installation Firm
55	Female	Jane	President of a Nonprofit
48	Male	Allen	Manager of Medical Software Developers
47	Male	William	Director of Admissions for a Medical School
47	Female	Juliet	Manager of Pharmaceutical Researchers

Validity and Reliability

Colton and Covert (2007) contend that validity is the extent to which a data-collection instrument measures what it is designed to measure. In qualitative research, validity also means the research procedures protect the accuracy of the data (Creswell, 2009). In Delphi research, validity is the level of consensus shared by expert participants (Skulmoski et al., 2007). The Delphi method promotes validity because participants have the opportunity to offer their insights, comment on contributions of others, and work toward achieving consensus (Heyman, 2010). External validity is limited because this was a qualitative study of a subset of the general population. Generalizability is limited to similar subsets of this population.

Reliability is the repeatability and consistency of results (Babbie, 2010). In qualitative research, reliability reflects a consistent approach employed through procedures that documents and evaluates data in the same manner (Creswell, 2009). Reliability in this study is enhanced by the five-person panel size (Heyman, 2010; Skulmoski et al., 2007). The Delphi technique addresses inter-rater reliability by using one facilitator to collect and code the data (Heyman, 2010) as well as participant-accuracy checking and peer de-briefing (Creswell, 2009).

Chapter Three Endnote

[1]The Delphi technique, in use since the 1950s for forecasting, solicits the input of a collection of experts. In that method, experts complete a questionnaire independently and anonymously. Their anonymous responses are circulated back sequentially to the experts to provide opportunities for them to rethink and revise their positions. This iterative process is deemed complete when the researcher's decision-criterion is met. The most common criterion for resolution is consensus.

The modified Delphi technique uses the same procedure, with a broader application than forecasting, and in this case, the application is understanding the phenomenon, mediated by e-mail technology to facilitate a time-efficient approach to reaching consensus and with concurrent versus sequential questionnaire circulation. The experts in this study were the participants. They understand the phenomenon better than anyone else. The experts were asked to review the written analysis of themes I derived from the data. I then asked them to provide feedback on the accuracy of the analysis, including what was correct, what was incorrect, and what was required to change to ensure the analysis accurately reflected their experiences. The experts were asked also what was missing. Their responses were compiled, then recirculated through email. Consensus was achieved at the completion of the second iteration.

[4]

The HIIT Experience

> It is a good morning exercise for a research scientist to discard a pet hypothesis every day before breakfast. It keeps him young.
>
> — Kondrad Lorenz (1903-1989)

The results are organized in three sections. The first part reports participant perceptions of the HIIT experience. Direct quotes from the interviews are offered throughout as substantiation. Several participants reported experiencing stress as they anticipate an upcoming workout. During the workout, participants recruit a great deal of inner focus and discipline, and after, participants report a sense of achievement and well-being. The second segment (Chapter 5) shares how the participants feel transformed by HIIT. They reported greater self-confidence, the belief that they can tackle grand challenges, and a confidence in practice and trial as a foundation for success. The third section (Chapter 6) examines their leadership styles. The participants generally employ a transformational leadership style. All said they lead by example. They are engaged through active participation in daily operations, stepping in whenever help is needed, mentoring, supporting, and coaching employees along their career paths, and empowering them in a safe, team-oriented environment. Chapter 6 reports the connections they perceive between their avid exercise in HIIT and their experiences in leadership.

How Leaders Experience HIIT

Participant's HIIT experiences fall into two categories. The first is achievement. Dimensions of achievement include well-being and exhilaration, pride, self-confidence, feeling part of an elite community of achievers, perseverance, understanding one's limits, and tackling enormous challenges. The second encompasses dimensions such as inner focus and discipline, pre-workout stress, a drive to compete against oneself, strategizing and prioritizing in light of one's limits, moving into the "right frame of mind" and into "the zone," and stepping outside one's comfort zone.

Achievement

The various participants began their training experiences in different ways and through different avenues. However, the passion with which they describe their experiences is remarkably similar. Among the five participants there were 57 comments concerning achievement of something important, which included 14 direct references plus several dimensions within that theme. These facets included 13 references to achievement within a community, 10 references to challenge, eight references to bolstered self-confidence, five references to well-being, four references to exhilaration, four references to developing perseverance, four references to pride, and three references to testing one's personal limits. For example, William notes feeling exhilaration and an elevated confidence in managing future challenges.

> *After, I feel exhilarated. I feel good. I feel rewarded. I feel like I've accomplished something that is significant. And frankly, whether it's the end of a marathon or the end of a WOD [workout of the day], I think the feeling is one of accomplishment and pride that I was able to do that. It's great; it was hard. You know if I can take that and manage that task, anything else the rest of the day will be pretty manageable.*

Within the context of discussing how HIIT has brought about personal change, Jane explained that the sense of accomplishment reinforces confidence in completing challenges successfully.

> *You know things that you think are impossible when you hear them the first time, [which are often in the form of] a task list [which is typically written on a white board at the start of the workout] of what you need to accomplish ... When you accomplish that [grueling and seemingly impossible set of exercises,] you get reinforcement that you can accomplish some pretty amazing things.*

Similarly, Juliet said "It has given me confidence to do the impossible."

Correspondingly, William made reference to understanding his limits and potential, and the importance of sharing that achievement with others in his community.

> *I think that having a sense of accomplishment and having an open mind to what my limits are, discovering new limits, being able to share that experience with the group as opposed to having a personal trainer one-on-one type of thing.*

The pride derived from achievement in these extreme workouts is consequent in part to belonging to an elite group, which in itself is a form of accomplishment. Allen said:

> *I have pride in accomplishments…space you know accomplishing things that maybe others haven't. That makes me feel good.*

Jane shared a similar sentiment:

> *So I think in that sense, it kind of made you feel a little more, maybe elite in a way as far as athletic and just being able to do some of these things that you knew nobody else was doing. I think that was kind of maybe a source of pride.*

Juliet also noted the perception of an elite community:

> *What it means [to be a HIIT athlete] is you're kind of a part of – a little bit of an elite group. People who really want to push the envelope and push the limits of their abilities versus going in and getting in your comfort zone. That's not why we work out [in HIIT] is [sic] to stay comfortable; we work out to constantly push ourselves. To be part of a group like that, it's a lot of fun.*

Greg offered that his fitness exceeds those who move heavy materials daily:

> *Well I have a lot of buddies who exercise but none of them could do what I do. I'm not the best person in the class. You know I just turned 40 years old. I'm not as fast as I used to be. I'm not as strong. I don't heal the same way. Compared to other guys my age, I'm heads and tails above them.... In my regular job I have installers and they have to lift stuff up all the time and every time there is something that is really heavy, I get the call. It's kind of funny when the boss comes in and he can out lift the guy who does the work every day.*

Taken together, achievement is seen as accomplishing exceptionally challenging tasks through which the participant gains self-confidence, an understanding of one's capabilities, a sense of pride, and satisfaction in achieving physical feats that grant the leader membership into an elite group. Moreover, the physical task accomplishment builds confidence in tackling any type of challenge as well as the perseverance to complete it. Jane reports:

> *What [HIIT has] done to change [me] is I think that [it developed] perseverance. I mean I was always pretty much – you know if I needed to do something, I could do it and kind of did that. But I think with the high-intensity and some of the challenges and some of the things you know that we do [in HIIT], it kind of really showed me that.*

Figure 1 depicts a conceptual interpretation of the experiences described by participants. Achievement is repre-

◉ Figure 1. Summary of HIIT Outcomes

Well-Being and
Exhilaration
(9 References)

Member of Elite
Community of
Achievers
(13 References)

Pride
(4 References)

Achievement
(57 References)

Self-Confidence
(8 References)

Perseverance
(4 References)

Understanding
Limits &Tackle
Insurmountable
Challenges
(13 References)

Figure 1 depicts the benefits HIIT athletes perceive from their training. A sense of achievement is central. Achievement is reinforced when practiced in community with others. Additional outcomes related to this achievement include pride, well-being and exhilaration, and heightened self-confidence. Athletes' achievement helped them learn that perseverance leads to desired results. They have a better understanding of their limits and a belief that they can tackle insurmountable challenges.

sented centrally because it may be a catalyst to the other benefits experienced by the participants. For example, well-being and pride could follow the completion of a challenging workout. Self-confidence, perseverance, and understanding limits, on the other hand, may be more cumulative because participants may need to experience success in several workouts before they notice the payback. Achievement also teaches the connection between hard work or perseverance, and triumph. The concepts portrayed in Figure 1 are conjecture, worthy of further exploration.

Inner Focus and Discipline

The sense of community is valued highly by all participants, however, they report that what is required during a workout is an inner focus that propels them through the extreme demands they face. This focus is described by participants as a solo experience, one in which they need to muster a remarkable level of inner strength to complete. Total references to inner focus and discipline were 40. Participants made nine references to being "in the zone," or tuning out those around them during their workouts. There were seven references to being in "the right frame of mind" to endure the workout, seven references to stepping "outside one's comfort zone," four references to feeling stress just before the workout begins, five references to the drive to compete against oneself, and two references to pushing oneself to such an extent that there is "nothing left in the tank."

To face the extreme challenge anticipated in a workout, three of the five participants described plotting a strategy just before the workout begins. Their strategizing entails analyzing what has worked in the past, determining how to pace themselves, and examining the structure of the workout to determine the best way to proceed given their individual strengths and weaknesses. Strategizing serves to motivate and orient them to the challenges they expect to face. Some excerpts are as follows. Allen said:

> *And then there is the point in time where you see what you have in front of you and you process it through in your mind. Now that we know most of all the exercises and what is involved so you know what it means when they put that on the board, you try to relate it to past experiences. To try to say I can do this because I did "this and this" before, and try to walk yourself through it, and then just attack it when it is time to start.*

Juliet shared the how she experiences pre-workout stress as follows:

> *I'm not going to have enough time. How long is it going to take me to do this? Sometimes you know it is going to take too long. We're not going to have enough time to finish this. So I think just having done this for so long, you know you kind of know what's on the board and kind of you know what to expect which helps but then also in some ways doesn't.* [LAUGHTER]

Jane reports assessing her athletic capacity so she can maintain her endurance:

> *I know I have to pace myself; I know how to do that. If it is a five round, I know. Okay, let all those people go real fast the first round. It's okay because I'll*

catch them by round four because they're going to die and I'll still be going. For me, I really learned my body.

Allen shared how he approaches different workouts with specific mindsets:

Now the exercises or the WODs can be different. They're very different if you have a set of tasks to do in a certain amount of time as opposed to an infinite amount of tasks in a certain amount of time. So the WODs that say do this and this and then you're done. And there are the ones that say you have the next forty minutes to do as many as you can. There are very different psychologies there to me and so I approach them in different ways. I think I do better when you have in front of you all the tasks you have to do. Those I do better because I can say this is what I have to do and then I can finish them. I have a little bit of a problem where it says do as many of these things you can do in thirty minutes because it just – it is harder to deal with psychologically, to me. The end is – or how many I do is up to me so it is almost more of a mental challenge that way.

William explained that the experience of completing extreme HIIT workouts taught the skill of prioritization.

I think it has really helped me focus in those areas of prioritizing. What is important? What's not? How do we get it done? What's the plan sort of to get it down? How are we going to know if it was successful or not? So I think that has probably changed a

> *great deal. Before this idea of [starting] high-intensity, where it was I got some exercise [that was not intense]. It felt good; it was nice. I sort of done [sic] it because I thought I was supposed to whereas in the last ten years or so with the more high-intensity stuff, I don't have to do it. I've made a conscious decision to want to do it and want to do it well. That's a big difference.*

A summary of themes related to training inputs is depicted in the figure on the next page. The arrows reflect conjecture concerning how these themes may be related.

Inner focus and discipline is one training input that seems interconnected with the others presented in Figure 2. Causality cannot be determined without further research. However, the two-directional arrows suggest possible influences that are bidirectional between inner focus and discipline and the other dimensions. Developing a sense of achievement and inner discipline in training seems to have brought about a sense of empowerment and personal transformation for these leaders, which is addressed in the next chapter.

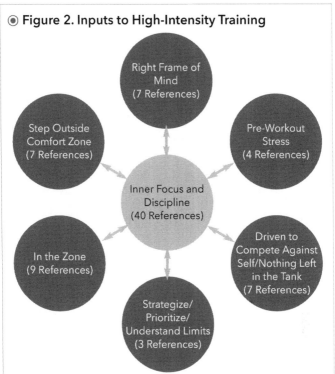

Figure 2. Inputs to High-Intensity Training

Right Frame of Mind (7 References)

Step Outside Comfort Zone (7 References)

Pre-Workout Stress (4 References)

Inner Focus and Discipline (40 References)

In the Zone (9 References)

Driven to Compete Against Self/Nothing Left in the Tank (7 References)

Strategize/ Prioritize/ Understand Limits (3 References)

Figure 2 portrays what athletes put into their training. All elements are interconnected; however, inner focus and discipline is a central dimension that propels them. Their discipline carries them through exercise regimens in which they must step outside their comfort zones to complete them successfully. They prepare themselves mentally before a workout, which is the meaning of the *right frame of mind*. They experience *pre-workout stress* as they prepare mentally to begin. They plan their approach to the workout, given the constraints of their physical capabilities and history of success in approaching similar exercise patterns, which is reflected in the *strategize/prioritize/understand limits* construct. They are driven to compete against themselves during a workout, to the point at which they perceive there is nothing left in the tank. Once they begin exercising, they report feeling *in the zone*.

[5]

THE HIIT TRANSFORMATION

> *By nature men are nearly alike; by*
> *practice, they get to be wide apart*
> — Confucius (551 BC- 479 BC)

How HIIT Changed Them

Beyond the physical demands and accomplishments, participants shared their perceptions concerning how HIIT changed them. One facet of the achievement motive and the desire for significant challenge is trusting that the process of practice, hard work, and trial leads to predictable outcomes. That process was viewed as catalyst to the development of self-confidence. Regarding mental challenge, Jane shared:

> *I think the whole thing was the mental challenge*
> *and knowing that most of it, probably eighty per-*
> *cent, is mental. Physically, I can do the work so-to-*
> *speak but sometimes what defeats you is your*
> *head... And then also kind of some of the chal-*

lenges, I use the box jump or even a handstand and it is like, "Why do I need to do that?" I'm just not going to do it because why do I need to do that. And I think being able to then kind of do it and say, "Oh okay, I did this and I can accomplish this." And then taking that into areas of my life knowing if I never try it, I'll never be successful at it. And so if I at least try it, you know, I may not be successful at first but you know that with repeated practice I will eventually become successful. I think that has carried over into my professional life as well as other areas in my personal life as well.

The following quote by Juliet illustrates the improved self-confidence brought about through HIIT.

I think the biggest thing that it has done is, it has given me a lot of confidence to do the impossible. What I mean when you look at some of the [HIIT] workouts, they're pretty intense and they're pretty long and you have to do sometimes like the "Filthy Fifty." You have to do fifty push-ups and fifty pull-ups and fifty this. I think most people look at that saying, "That's insane. That's crazy. That's not possible." It gave me a sense of wow. I can do the impossible. And that's quite uplifting when you think about it that I can do something like this.... So it kind of extends your way of thinking, I think into life too. I can do things. I'm not limited now.

A related dimension is recruiting one's competitive drive to tackle the insurmountable. William reports:

Then the other thing I would say is it helped me re-

ally refocus this energy, competitive drive in terms of my getting better. You know I care less about what other people do although I want them to do well. But you know I don't care if I lift more than other people in the gym. I care if I'm lifting more now than I did a year ago based on good technique, practice, etc.

In sum, participants report favorable changes from their HIIT. They are more confident, feel able to tackle difficult tasks, and trust that with practice and trial they can achieve hard-to-reach goals. Figure 3 on the next page highlights these relationships.

The athletes' sense of accomplishment provides a heightened sense of well-being, pride, confidence, belongingness, perseverance, self-awareness of capabilities, and a belief in their capacity to conquer challenge. They employ self-discipline and a mindset that equips them to endure demanding exercise regimens. HIIT not only transformed them into individuals more self-assured than before, it also helped them to believe in their capabilities and trust the processes required to achieve desired outcomes in their life endeavors. The next chapter reports emergent themes concerning participants' leadership styles.

⊙ Figure 3. How High-Intensity Exercise Changed Them

Self-
Confident
(8 references)

Can
Tackle the
Insurmountable
(8 references)

Practice,
Trial, and Failures Lead
to Success
(9 references)

Personal Changes from High-Intensity Exercise

Figure 3 depicts the ways in which participants felt transformed through their HIIT training. They reported noteworthy gains in self-confidence, which transfers beyond their gym experiences, infusing self-assurance into their work and personal lives. Related to a self-confident comport is a trust in their ability to tackle challenges they once believed were impossible. The final change is a life view that embraces failure, trial, and practice as given waypoints on a path to success.

[6]

LEADERSHIP STYLES OF AVID EXERCISERS

Management is doing things right; leadership is doing the right things.

— Peter Drucker (1909-2005)

How They Lead

Many dimensions of transformational leadership were salient in the participants' descriptions of their approaches to leadership. They lead by example, empower employees, and rely on a team orientation. All mentioned that selecting high-quality employees is a necessary input to lead well. One interesting finding, which may reflect the unique culture of HIIT, is the use of measurement as a motivational tool. Part of the interview protocol probed transactional dimensions of leadership, including the importance of the chain of command. These leaders tend to recognize its importance, however, they do so enlisting assumptions that fit better in the transformational model. The following sections share these results in greater depth.

Lead by Example

All participants said they lead by example (29 references were made among the five participants). They set examples either through demonstrating their experiences with employees' work functions or modeling the comportment and passion of one who is successful in the given field. Regardless, they engage through active participation. For example, Greg and William mention setting the standards they expect of employees. Greg explained:

> *I try and lead by example you know as far as being a role model. I'm the first one in; I'm the last one to leave at work. Which is the fun part of being boss, you get to work harder than everybody else.... I've never asked any of my employees [to do anything I would not be willing to perform] and I tell them that when I hire somebody. I say, "I'll never ask you to do anything that I couldn't do or haven't done myself."*

A similar sentiment, expressed by both Jane and William, conveyed a willingness to step in whenever help is needed. The focus is on achieving goals, but not a specific employment title, such as CEO. William said:

> *And last but not least this idea that we're all part of the team and no one is bigger than the team so we all pitch in and do different things. If that means tomorrow I have to make copies, I'll make copies. If tomorrow I have to go see the president ..., then I'll go see the president... There is no task too big or too small; rather they're all tasks as a team we have to accomplish. I'm as capable of making copies as*

our secretary.... So whatever the duty calls for on that given day that is sort of what we do.

Jane offered:

I don't expect things from other people that I don't expect of myself. I'm always willing to roll up my sleeves and do whatever needs to be done. I think when people see that they appreciate it and they trust what you're saying because your actions are meeting with your words and they are motivated by that and they try to excel in a similar way.

William also explained how he sets standards through personal conduct.

But I guess what I would say is to the extent that I can remain focused, disciplined, hold myself accountable to high standards, high outcomes, I think that is a good example, if you will, for the other teammates.

Another dimension of leading by example is mentoring employees along their career paths. For example, Juliet models creative problem solving for employees.

I love problem solving. I love seeing – If there is ever a problem or if there is ever something you have to figure out, which there is always to figure out ... I always come up with really unique strategies.

Allen models how to buffer employees from organizational problems so they can focus on their work.

> *I think I serve as a role model to other people who have been promoted to managers, people who are in other departments. I've gotten feedback that I am in many cases. Anyone on my team that has an interest in going on a management path instead of a technical path, I would like to think they emulate me and especially from the people part of it. I try to act as the buffer between the business requirements and the hard and fast budget issues and the people actually doing the work. If I can absorb some of that worry and some of the deadline restrictions and things like that, then I feel good about that. I think that is what people want to emulate about me.*

The leader's passion is another dimension of example-setting. Juliet said:

> *Science is about coming up with new inventions, new cures to help mankind. It is not all about, "I developed this and good for me. I know I'm special."*

Jane commented:

> *...but it is having that passion for the population that we're serving and really kind of walking the walk. It is not just talking the talk; it is also walking the walk and showing that passion and that commitment. I think it inspires others to want to achieve the same thing. Whether it be, I want to eventually be an executive director of an organization or I want to be a supervisor or whatever. What do I need to do in order to be able to do that?*

The participants pitch in when needed at work, modeling the passion they feel toward their work. Their knowledge of the tasks they ask their employees to complete suggests an empathetic disposition as well as an understanding of how to plan for and execute organizational outcomes. One aspect of the dynamic governing their communication with employees is the respect they hold for those reporting to them.

High Quality Employees - A Necessary Input

Common to all participants is the view that a leader needs high-quality employees to function effectively (seven comments in total). Dimensions of this theme include working well with others, a willingness to learn, an attitude of commitment to the organization, and contributing to the creative and innovative tasks of the organization.

Allen explained:

> *I hire people that I believe can be self-managed. Not that they don't need a manager but that they can work in a group.*

Jane and Greg offered that motivated employees make the leader's tasks easier. Jane said:

> *I think for me every job I take, everything I do, is a learning opportunity. And so if people come in with that kind of an open mind to learning and those things are changing especially in the environments we work in nowadays....You don't have to be young or inexperienced but it is just that openness and willingness to learn, and be open*

and respecting that other people have knowledge that you can benefit from.

Greg stated:

If they don't want to be there, I don't want them there. If they're just there for the check, we don't want them there. That's [an employee] who is never going to have any loyalty to you. He's going to leave for fifty cents more an hour to somebody else. You know he's going to feel that you owe him something and that's not somebody you want on your staff. So if you can find people who actually want to be part of your organization, you'll do a lot better.

Allen believes the software-development field in which he works tends to attract good employees. Those employees are necessary inputs to companywide innovation.

In this business it is not that hard to stimulate people. You know to be innovative because that's part of what we do. If we're not innovative then you know we're not going to be competitive either as individuals within our careers or competitive as a company with other companies. It is not that hard to do that.

Participants acknowledge the importance of talent on their teams. They ensure they surround themselves with employees who are interested in learning, bring their talents to their organizations, and can function autonomously. The next section shares how participants empower the capable employees whom they hire.

Employee Empowerment and Team-Orientation

Perhaps a corollary to high-quality employees is empowerment, soliciting input, making learning opportunities available to prepare employees for personal and organizational goal attainment, and viewing employee teams as the most effective path toward goal attainment. Sixty two comments supported the creation of this theme. Greg acknowledged the shared vulnerability of managers and employees.

> *They understand we're all in it together. When they succeed, I succeed.*

The participants see themselves as facilitators working with talented teams. Employees were frequently seen as team members by participants. Comments such as "I stress collaboration within the group"; "I'm pretty fortunate that I am the leader, director, of this team. I guess I would say I deal with them as team mates"; "They understand that you're there for the team; you're not just the boss that sits in a room somewhere and collects a check"; and "I am somebody that really likes to set up self-managed groups" were comments emblematic of their regard for their teams. Juliet acknowledged the need for employee buy-in for successful goal attainment.

> *And you can get people to engage, [to] have some ownership and [because of that buy-in that they] have ... you know [they will] take it and also then support it.*

Similarly, Allen said employees will be

> *more invested in the path to the goal. And they can come to work more fulfilled as opposed to just*

being told what to do all the time. You know they can own the process.

One dimension of empowerment that emerged is accepting multiple paths to the same goal. Jane said,

You still have to get the outcomes but there're a lot of different ways that people get to that point and get those outcomes.

Jane added:

Here's the outcome; this is what we need to achieve. "How are we going to get there? How are you going to get there? How can we accomplish this goal?" There is not one way; there are a lot of different ways to get there.

Multiple paths to the same outcome was a theme mentioned commonly among managers of professionals. However, Greg, who works in the warehouse delivery and installation field, relies heavily on well-defined procedures and processes with limited-to-no use of employee discretion. When innovation and creativity are required, however, Greg employs the team approach as well. He provided the following two examples:

Basically, what we did is we all got together and said, "Here's a new product we're going to be working with. Let's all go out and learn about it and then we'll come here and we'll get together and figure out ways we can do this a little better." So we went through the wall training with the factory and came back to our shop. The first thing [an employee] said is: "Why in the world would they use a miter saw to cut the trim? Why wouldn't they just have a vinyl trim cutter cut it?" ... And in about fifteen minutes we had a vinyl trim cutter that saved probably thirty percent of the time on the job by being able to tote a cordless tool around, which weighed three pounds instead of dragging a hundred foot extension cord around the job site with you and a power miter saw and having to vacuum it up after you're done....And we developed a crown cutting clamp, which is a clamp that allows you to trim the metal channels that hold the wall in place with one person. Before, you would have two people that would have to cut this thing. You'd have a twelve foot piece of metal that weighed about twenty-five to thirty pounds. One [employee] is holding it and one [employee] cutting it. You have one [employee] whose whole job is just to hold onto this thing all day long. While you're paying this [employee], he's just holding onto this thing while another [employee] cuts it. That's ridiculous so we developed a clamp that lets one [employee] do it and now that other [employee] can go out and produce. It's a matter of kind of getting together and looking at process.

Juliet considers the quality of team work superior to that of individual work.

But it is not just me by myself because I know I only have a limited amount of knowledge. I love working in a team. I love bringing everybody's specialty into the mix so ... I love them to see my point of view but then I say, "How would you solve this?" Because I mean it has been kind of shown that when you have

> *a group effort solving a problem, usually the solution is much better than an individual's solution. You know it is better thought out. It is better.*

Participants view goal clarity and even team vision creation and planning as essential prerequisites to entrusting employees with decision authority.

For example, William offered:

> *I want my team to understand what our goals are. So I guess I would say I spend a lot of time trying to work with the team to make sure we understand what our goals are, our objectives, what our vision is. And to be clear what we are going to do as a team and to be clear what we're not going to do.*

William also stated:

> *I would say to a great extent, we spend a lot of time thinking about, what do we want to be as a team? What do we want to accomplish as a team? How individually as team members can we promote that? What's involved and required to be a good team member? Is it professional skill development? Is it a personal development? Is it time away from the office to go explore other areas?*

Juliet said:

> *I give them the crux of the idea or the problem we need solved and then we work together as a team to solve it.... If I start telling them what to do then they are a pair of hands; they're going to disen-*

gage. I always need people engaged. If they're engaged, you'll get the best productivity. You'll get the best creativity. If they disengage forget it; they're just a pair of hands.

Participants do not view empowerment as relinquishing their managerial responsibility. Allen said:

I don't think a self-managed group is just to say, "Hey, go off and do what you need." There is constant follow-up and monitoring of the facilitation as opposed to dictating what they should do and that way they're more invested in the process.

William stressed the importance of on-going communication with individual team members.

I try and interact pretty regularly with every team member. "What is going on today? What's up? What's down? What's good? What's bad?" And to not be afraid to make changes on the spot that we're a pretty fluid organization in terms of aligning and realigning goals based on where we are.

Ten references were made to another dimension of employee empowerment, which is providing opportunities to learn, grow, and perform. Allen sees learning new skills as an opportunity to help the company as well as to enrich the employee's experience.

I encourage them to learn new skills. They can step outside of the box that they're in. Yeah, they might be happy being a quality assurance engineer but every once in a while when we need help coding

> *software, maybe there are some things you can learn that you can help out with you and enrich your daily experience, even if you didn't want to be a software engineer. So I try to encourage them by finding a way to enrich their everyday experience.*

Juliet develops employee presentation skills. If employees need help, the participant will intervene, but not before empowering them to tackle the challenge themselves.

> *You know I support them because I give them the opportunities. There are a lot of scientists – Well there are a lot of directors or vice-presidents who just want to present everything and they don't give their subordinates the opportunity to present.... If they start getting into trouble or start getting nervous, I'll jump in and help them out a little bit. But that's how I do it. I kind of help train them that way.*

Other participants ask employees to research new approaches to their work, or even to benchmark other industries to find innovative approaches to work processes. Allen shared:

> *Really, just making it available and constantly stressing that just because this is what we did for the last ten or fifteen years and this is the technology we used – you know go out and Google stuff. I mean we have a vast amount of knowledge at our fingertips; we don't have to go to a library. Find out what is going on in the industry.*

William shared his approach as well:

We actually spend a lot of time on that [employee empowerment]. I think there are two ways. One is pretty general on an ongoing basis, which is we look outside of our industry to try to get ideas and information. We try and learn from Google how they select employees to figure out what we might learn about selecting future [clients]. We look at social service agencies to see how they excite people about service projects and so on. I think one way is we're always looking outside the industry to try to find innovation that's number one.

William formalizes the education process that empowers employees to pursue any area of interest to them. Employees are required to report what they learned quarterly to their teammates. He shared:

Every member gets two days a month to do whatever they want. In the [office], outside the [office], at home, go on a fieldtrip, or whatever they want – to work on a project or challenge that they have personally with their work or that we have as a group. And so they could go watch videos for a day. They could stay at home and read articles. They could go talk to people they know in other industries. They could do whatever they want for two days a month. And by the way they're required to do that; it is not sort of optional. Which they love and so making them do it isn't difficult. But we have quarterly process meetings. At each process meeting you have to report what you did for two days, what project you're working on, and what progress you're making. It has led to some amazing efficiencies for our group. Because when you give people

> *a chance to work on challenges that they face in their daily life and/or see reoccurring, and then give them the freedom to go figure out ways to do it, they come back with some pretty cool ideas, so that's probably the best thing we've ever done here in the last seven or eight years, the idea of two days a month. You leave the office and go figure out how we make something better. How you do that, I don't care. But again we spend a lot of time doing that.*

When employees learn new skills, Allen recognizes a mutual benefit derived from developing employees. Providing stretch goals to talented employees reduces the manager's workload. It also develops the skill base for the employees.

> *Now, I can say that that people who are interested in a certain career path and if I can help them do that, the people that I really advocate are the ones that take on additional responsibilities maybe outside of their role, maybe somebody who takes some pressure off of me. Maybe they go to a meeting or take on a recurring [meeting] that I would normally go to but I don't have the capacity for and they start with learning some things. I like to identify folks like that and kind of use that to allow them to progress and so indirectly that ends up being kind of [a] reward.*

For non-professional employees, Greg takes a summative approach through financial incentives.

> *But if you give them the opportunity to make more, they will find a way to perform a little better and make more money.*

Two final dimensions of empowerment and team orientation include a focus on employees' strengths and valuing their individual differences. William said

> I try to deal with them from contexts that are important to them. Meaning I try to understand their situation: What are the drivers of their motivation? Is it projects? Is it outcomes? Is it relationships?

Within the team context, participants report a mixed set of activities to keep employees engaged. With an empathetic regard for employees, Juliet considers it productive to build upon the inherent strengths of individual team members.

> I really like working in groups and using people's strengths. I know my weaknesses very well and so when I manage people, I manage their strengths. I do not waste time on saying, "You know what? You've got to get better at this." No-no-no, we're going to drive your strengths and you know what? Your weaknesses, we'll deal with it but you know what I know my weaknesses....But when I manage I manage people['s] strengths. You know what? I don't want someone to waste their time if they're not good at [SIGHS] I don't know. I don't want to waste their time with them doing that. Do what you do the best. That's how I do – I always manage to strengths.

William aims to tailor motivational tactics to reinvigorate employees to perform at their best when their positions are the most demanding.

> *I'm trying to find ways to put people in situations to be successful. If that means sending them to a conference, great, if that means sending them home for a day to think about out-of-the-box solutions, if it means going to spend a day at Google to see how they solve problems, if it means taking a day off to go [to a theme park] with their kids to sort of reenergize – I'm always trying to think about how do we keep our team happy? So that when the time comes, they can be very focused and very driven, which you know is a lot of hours. I would lastly say this idea of balance. How do we keep the team balanced? I want them to work hard but I also want them to play hard so that when they're here we're focused and we're having some fun and working hard but that they come energized and excited.*

In summation, participants empower their employees. They share decision-making authority. They view themselves as facilitators, and depend on their teams to solve problems and make creative decisions. They let employees determine their own path to a shared goal, even if that route deviates from the leader's thinking because they appreciate the importance of employee ownership to achieve creative solutions. Part of empowerment is providing opportunities for employee growth to bolster skill levels and to master new perspectives to apply in problem-solving. They encourage their employees to share what they learn to promote learning and engagement within the organizational community. Related to empowerment is goal setting, which these HIIT leaders connect to measurement and motivation.

Measurement as a Motivational Tool

Monitoring and control comprise one of the four functions of management. Measurement is central to HIIT as well, and emerges as an important theme in 64 comments offered in the interviews. Participants go beyond standard policies and monitor performance as a means of coaching and inspiring employees. They use measurement to facilitate timely communication, contingency planning, and feedback, and they connect what they measure to employee rewards.

William and Jane explicitly emphasized the importance of measuring what matters. William offered:

> *I don't want to do something just for the sake of doing it. Sometimes, it forces you to be creative in how you're going to measure things. But we need to keep score, I think. These are finite resources. We've got to be smart; we've got to be efficient. Are we doing a good job of shepherding these resources, successful outcomes or not?*

Jane measures outcomes versus activities that are disconnected to goals.

> *My thing is that if you've got the outcomes, I really don't care where you're at every day.*

Much like a HIIT workout that posts prescribed levels of performance and the athletes' scores or times against those targets, three participants keep score in the office to track performance and to troubleshoot. William refers to "keeping score," Allen uses the term "rally," and Jane uses "challenges."

For example, William explained:

> But I think the bigger way for us is we keep score.
> We have objectives for the day, for the week, for
> the month, for the quarter.... And they're all listed;
> we have a big board in our storeroom of what
> those key indicators are.... The team has to con-
> tribute to, to achieve them although some people
> have lead roles in some areas and not others....
> There is a big scoreboard that says how we're
> doing relative to customer service measured by
> evaluations from the [measure removed for
> anonymity]. The goal there is ninety-nine percent
> satisfaction, so if we're at seventy-two percent for
> this month, that's not good and we color code
> them. Black is static, green is improving and red is
> below average.... We know what numbers we're
> after so there is no ambiguity about are we good
> or bad. We know that the turnaround rate ...should
> be forty-eight hours. We know if it is seventy-two
> hours that we've got a breakdown somewhere. If
> we're at thirty-six hours that's good and we're
> ahead of the schedule as well.

As mentioned in the above quote, Juliet shared that
goal clarity focuses employee efforts and also empowers
employees to monitor themselves against those measures.

> I give them clear goals, clear guidelines and clear
> expectations.... [There] cannot be in [sic] any gray
> area. It has to be black and white....It is very precise
> [in writing].... It is like you need to do A, B, C, D, and
> E. And then you have to go through and say, "How
> did I do on A?" You know I was eighty percent ef-

fective on A. You grade yourself and it is funny when you ask people and they have certain goals or certain areas they have to achieve and you ask them to grade themselves. They're usually more critical on themselves than you are.

Allen uses the term "rally" to convey score keeping, and keeps the focus on performance through stand-up meetings, capped at 15 minutes, to empower teammates to prioritize, help a teammate in trouble, and problem solve.

I actually ask them once a day to keep up on this rally [tracking software]... I don't want them to spend a lot of time on that but I do ask them to do that once a day. And then once every morning, I have the group. The team comes to work and we have a stand-up meeting. We stand up because we don't want it to be a long, drawn-out meeting. Fifteen minutes is the limit but I want to hear from every person, "What did they do yesterday? What are they going to do today? What's blocking them if anything?" I want to hear those three things and really nothing else. The team manages that. It is not necessarily that I want to hear it but I want the team to hear it. If somebody is having a problem the team can collapse in and pull that person in and help them. Maybe somebody is running behind and somebody else is ahead of schedule, so everybody works to complete what we committed to at the beginning of the iteration by the end of the iteration and we commit to it as a team.

Allen also measures progress against incremental goals. Incremental measures support staying on course and steady progress toward goals.

> *And what I like to do is I like to divide things up into incremental goals...instead of looking at the whole problem and having it be overwhelming... I set up two-week time boxes to where we have specific pieces, features of the software, that we need to do. We try to make our biweekly goals and if we make all of our biweekly goals or even if we miss a few of them, that we're not having to worry about catching up at the end or working long hours and scrambling to finish by the final deadline.*

Measurement Tied to Rewards

Participants said they reward only exceptional performance. Jane said:

> *I think you know there are people who go above and beyond and I think that's where they deserve that recognition.*

William offered:

> *I think everyone knows Monday through Friday, nine to five, has to be a good worker. But what about that activity on Saturday afternoon or Friday night or doing things sort of above and beyond?*

Jane, Allen, and Juliet said they do not have the purview to offer financial rewards. However, Greg, empowered with such authority, devises compensation programs that reward employees financially for exceptional performance.

> *Rewards are almost always financial. It is performance-based. If the [employees] beat their goal times*

and they do a good job, they'll be rewarded finan-cially. We give a Christmas bonus. One of our [em-ployees] just had a baby so he had to take a week off and we got him a three hundred dollar gift card to help buy some diapers and that sort of thing.

Much like creatively tailoring a gift to a new father in the example above, most participants develop creative non-monetary rewards that tap into the unique needs of individual employees. Jane said:

The struggle being is that we don't have the funds. I always wish I could give this person a bonus or I could give them more money or whatever, although that is not always what people want. And so being kind of creative in how you provide rewards.

Jane added also that she uses monthly challenges to achieve an outcome.

And so then we would track people's outcomes for that month and based on certain criteria, we would score them. And then we would give the person who had the highest placement rate [a reward].... I would give them a day off because it was – It was costing me but it wasn't costing me anything out of pocket, so-to-speak.

Other examples cited by Jane, William, and Allen in-clude offering flextime or sending employees home early or for a long weekend when they have worked hard or ac-complished challenging goals. William mentioned that many employees value flextime over monetary rewards.

Another non-monetary reward is the provision of training and growth opportunities.

Allen Said:

> *Our training budgets have been kind of low the last couple of years because we've gone through a transition of ownership but I still try to find some opportunities for people to do web training or things like that.*

Juliet, who manages scientists, described growth opportunities for employees to present their research to "actually invest in people in ways they know they're benefitting."

Failure is Valuable

Goal achievement is valued by participants, however, Juliet emphasized value in failure; either in the form of mistakes made by the leader or by employees, because lapses are a path to growth and may even lead to discoveries.

> *... what is the key to success in leadership? I think all my failures have made me stronger. They were learning experiences. I've had several of them, many hundreds of them [LAUGHS]. I mean you don't go into science to have one hundred percent success rate. Ninety-nine percent of the stuff you work on, fails. If you want to be a failure, go into science. [LAUGHTER] A lot of stuff doesn't work. When it does work, it changes the world and so [LAUGHS]... if they make a mistake, you know*

> what? Everybody makes mistakes. There're always failures. You never nail them to the wall - that or the cross because of that.

Juliet, Allen, and William mentioned the need to create a safe environment; fear is counter-productive. William offered:

> I just don't think you can motivate people out of fear. I think we motivate out of interest, out of success, out of a genuine passion for doing things together. And again, knock on wood, it has worked fairly well.

Juliet said:

> I really never punish. I don't think it is ever a good idea to ever punish anybody. I've been punished and all that does is lead to disengagement. If you punish someone you want them to leave.

Acknowledging that frustration can result from employee mistakes, Greg reported the drawbacks of expressing anger.

> I found that yelling and screaming doesn't really do a whole lot except turn people off.... You can scream till you're blue in the face and all it's going to do is turn people off and put them in a bad mood. It's not going to help the situation.

William offered the use of goal setting for punishment prevention.

> *I've not had to do a lot of punishment because the goals are pretty clear; the vision is pretty clear.*

Greg, who supervises non-professional employees, focuses on studying the root causes of a mistake and discussing the consequences emanating from it to spur learning.

> *In most cases when people make a mistake, it's just that; it's a mistake. Sometimes, they know better and they're in a hurry. It's Friday afternoon at two o'clock when it's sunny outside... You have to sit back and illustrate to them, "What happened? Why did we do it this way? Let's backtrack and figure it out." At that point you can kind of dissect what the situation was and then you can illustrate to them. Now, we have to go back to that job site; we have to send a truck, two [employees] and that truck costs about a hundred and twenty five dollars to send out to somebody's job site and two people. We'll add it up and it is about a four hundred or five hundred dollar mistake. "What are we going to do next time?"*

An additional example of studying root causes involves team problem solving. Allen said:

> *...if there is a process issue we have that is blocking us, I really want—as opposed to me setting down an edict of this is how we solve this process issue or some kind of a defect that is blocking in our process—I want the group to figure it because that way the group owns it and they can change it accordingly to come up with a solution of "Why are we not performing the way we should?"*

Greg, Jane, and Allen noted the importance of addressing problems immediately. For example, Jane reports:

> *Early in my career, you know I had kind of an issue of confrontation. I didn't really want to rock the boat. "Hey, they're doing okay. There are a couple things but I don't want to really go there because it might be uncomfortable." I'm now in the mode of no surprises. If there is something that is bothering me about the way someone is performing, I let them know as soon as possible and I let them know in a very positive manner.*

A unique feature of this form of HIIT is the "personal record" (called the "PR" among participants) and the use of measurement to rouse employees to perform best. Greg shared:

> *My favorite workout, ["The Workout"], my best score ever is three hundred seventy one. I haven't gone below three hundred in five years. And I'm getting old and I know there's going to be a day that I'll – I'll hit that three hundred mark and start dropping below it. But you know you look at it the same way. We've got a job to do. We've got a workout to do. Let's see how we're going to do it and what's our strategy? And let's get to it. So that sense of achievement is the parallel [between HIIT and leadership] I see.*

Transactional leaders focus on rewards and punishment to achieve employee compliance. However, these leaders avoid punishment, and focus instead on inspiring employees. They set clear goals, measure what matters, focus on outcomes versus activities, and monitor closely progress toward goal attainment. What is measured is connected to rewards; the focus on significant goals and measures keeps these leaders focused on what is meaningful in the work of their employees and teammates. Important in bureaucratic organizations, the chain of command may not seem fitting in an exploration of transformational leadership. However, the next section uncovers the non-mechanistic perspective toward the chain of command, which was held by the HIIT leaders interviewed.

The Role of the Chain of Command

The final facet of leadership style was drawbacks and contributions the chain of command provides. Questions concerning the chain were part of the interview protocol, designed to probe for transactional behaviors. Responses were consistent with a transformational mindset instead. Participants said they are not concerned with title or position for ego gratification, nor do they want to focus on organizational politics. Juliet cautioned that the chain of command is a drawback if important information does not reach top management.

> I don't feel like the chain of command should be filtering.... But you really have to tell them [top executives] exactly what's going on. That's when big companies really get issues. Because when things rise to the top, things get filtered. You only hear the good stuff and that's when big [reference to industry removed] companies get potentially damaging because you're holding back certain information that could really affect the project.

Despite these downsides, participants cited significant benefits of the chain as a coordinating mechanism. The chain of command communicates organizational and stakeholder expectations, determines organizational priorities and efficient resource allocation, and organizes communication. "If there is an issue, someone knows exactly when to call or who to call," offered Greg. William expressed how the chain provides direction within the context of organizational priorities.

> I don't want a chain of command where people ask me, "Can I go to the bathroom? Can I make this copy? Can I do this project?" But rather I want a team that says, "I made a go of this; I tried it and it didn't work. What do we do next?" I want them taking some chances but relative to chain of command, I want them to know, "Does it fit within our vision? Does it fit within our resources?"... I want people to understand their roles and how we advance the organization but I don't want and we don't get into you know, "This memo needs four or five or six signatures."

Relative to clarifying organizational priorities, Juliet added:

> And if you have ten things you have to do, this person can't be "Okay, we're going to do all kinds of things at once and we're going to get them done at once." Everything has the same priority – you can't manage like that. When it comes to chain of command, my vice-president has to have a clear understanding of what's the most important, critical thing. And that has to come down, if all of a

sudden your chain of command is sending the wrong messages and you're working on the wrong things, people like me who are super creative and can do a lot of things will then get super burned out because they're working on everything at once and there are not priorities. Or they work on everything at once and it takes forever because you can't work on everything at once.

Allen sees the chain as less relevant to modern business models.

There're more people that you report to than just your boss is what I'm trying to say. On a functional level so I don't spend a lot of time worrying about this person told me this and I'm going to go over this person's head and stuff like that because I don't really think in a modern business – at least at my level that is the most important thing. If it is a little bit redundant or ambiguous to who I should listen to? I don't really worry about that that much. I just make sure we have agreement among everyone and that our process is smooth. So it is not a big stickler for me.

One might expect transactional leaders to emphasize the chain of command, and presume that the transactional leader may rely on the hierarchy and positional authority to establish context for quid-quo-pro exchanges. However, these participants view the hierarchy favorably, as a mechanism to assist and empower employees. They use the chain to support, not stifle, their teams. So far, participants' experiences as HIIT athletes, including their personal transformation, and perceptions of their leadership behaviors have been described. The next chapter contains the connections participants identify between HIIT and leadership.

[7]

Parallels in HIIT and Leadership

> *Perhaps the only moral trust with any certainty in our hands is the care of our own time.*
>
> — Edmund Burke (1729-1797)

How HIIT and Leadership Intersect

Participants cited several dimensions when asked to consider connections between their HIIT and leadership experiences. They noted a parallel sense of achievement and desire to achieve within a community. They never feel satisfied and they are driven to push forward continually to accomplish more. A common feeling of passion, dedication, focus, discipline, and drive to keep progressing was present in both. Time management skills and management efficiencies were part of both, as were openness to risk taking and change, and tackling insurmountable tasks. A parallel view of failure as a path to achievement was cited. The final commonality was measurement.

Parallel Sense of Achievement and Goal Attainment

Achievement was a noteworthy theme in participants' descriptions of their experiences in HIIT. It surfaced also when they discussed overlaps. Greg reports:

> *Well, both high-intensity exercise and leadership focus around achievement. You can't really be a leader without constantly looking for achievement. Whether it is financial or a certain project that had to be done a certain way. The same thing happens with CrossFit [HIIT]. There're workouts that you get better and better at and there are some you're just not good at. You try and try and try and you conquer them.*

The notion of pushing one's limit is a dimension of achievement that emerged in both. Jane added:

> *I think there is definitely a connection. I think for me, I've always whether it be in – I've always, I've never really been satisfied. It's like I'm always looking and pushing myself a little bit more in no matter what I do.... So I think for me that I've always been that kind of person, never really satisfied. Sometimes, it's a curse but I'm never really satisfied. There's got to be more. You can learn more. You can do more. You can achieve more. It's not just about achieving. I think it is about pushing myself in doing more, doing better, and doing different things.*

Part of achievement is accomplishing insuperable tasks. Completing those tasks requires an openness and self-confidence to undertake the challenge. Allen mentions the drive is expressed within the work community.

> I think it goes back to that first question: How do you think [HIIT] has changed you? It has made me more open to seemingly insurmountable tasks. And I have a desire to spread that feeling amongst the people that work with me.

Mental Grit and Passion

William explained the common mindset required in both HIIT and leadership. Again, the idea of its application within community emerges as a dimension.

> *I think the reality is there is a lot of overlap. So I think some of the words that describe that overlap would be things like focus, discipline, time management, efficiency, community that is collaborative. So I think there is really a lot of overlap relative to the skills one has in exercise and leadership. I think there are a lot of the same qualities. You know some of those I just listed, I think, are good examples.*

Juliet notes the common role of passion in propelling the leader or avid exerciser through the extreme demands of the workout or the profession.

> *I think the only way to get through these [HIIT] WODs is to be highly energized and passionate because they're so hard. They're so grueling and if you give up, you give up. So you have to be super charged, super passionate, super in-the-moment.*

And that is what I do in my science. I'm super charged, super passionate, and super in-the-moment. And so I just see a direct correlate between the two.

Risk-Taking and Change

Jane and Juliet noted a parallel openness to taking risks. Jane said:

You know maybe they [leaders] are high risk takers. They tend to be some leaders in their field. You take a look at a lot of the scientists who tend to do things. A lot of them are rock wall climbers or these ultra-athletes. They know the dedication that is involved in their passion. But they also have that same dedication to their physical exercise, too. So I see that a lot. I mean you look at a lot of these people and that's what they do. So I think if you have this really great passion on one hand, it kind of shadows a lot of other parts of your life.

In addition to risk taking, Juliet noted the breakthroughs that result from failure as well as an openness to change:

I see other people who gripe about not getting to where they want to be but then they don't do anything about it. And that part drives me crazy because there are so many things you can do to help you get to the next level. It is wherever you want in life [LAUGHS]. You know I think education, doing new things, finding new friends – I mean doing all these things are really important.

If you keep doing the same thing and keep getting the same answer, that is science, right? You experiment. If again and again, you get the same answer, well, you've got to change something [LAUGHS]. You know it is hard to change. It is scary to change. You could fail. So I think everybody could be great, successful, passionate leaders. I think there is some self-limiting going on there.

Measurement

Finally, participants found that measurement and score-keeping are common to both HIIT and leadership. Setting clear goals provides something to measure. William calls this intention or purposefulness.

I would say again some of the same sort of goals or overlaps [occur in HIIT and leadership]. You know this idea of outcomes matter, keeping score, having a clear vision of what I want to accomplish, being able to do it in a reasonable established time frame, I think are very important. I guess maybe if I could use one word to describe it, I guess it would be something like purposefulness – if that is even a word. What are we going to do in this hour? How do I see it playing out? What are the outcomes? Why are we doing it? Why is it important? How does it contribute to the other things around us? So to me whether it is a one hour WOD or a one hour meeting, this idea of being purposeful or intentional. It is not random. It is not haphazard. There is a clear agenda. What are we going to get done? How are we going to get it done? What is success going to look like on the other end?

Related to intentionality and goal setting is measurement. Leaders measure to motivate employees at work, and note its use also in the context of HIIT. Jane noted

> *In my professional environment there is so much cross over. Every day I see things in how you motivate an athlete versus how you motivate an employee.*

Greg's quote concerning the PR, mentioned in the section on motivating through measurement in the previous chapter, supports parallel views of measurement, albeit metrics pertaining to "The Workout" or the tasks in one's organization. The dimensions common to the HIIT experience and leadership are summarized in the figure on the next page.

⊚ **Figure 4. Parallel Dynamics Experienced Both in HIIT and Leadership**

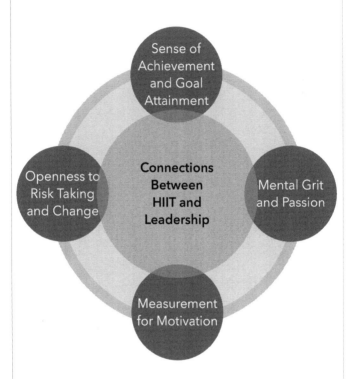

Figure 4 illustrates the connections participants reported between HIIT and leadership. In both there is delight in achievement and goal attainment. Mental grit and passion are qualities that propel them in both domains. HIIT and leadership both require an open mindset that welcomes risk-taking and change. Measurement, used as a tool to motivate themselves and others, is the final dimension common to both HIIT and leadership.

[8]

IMPLICATIONS AND FUTURE RESEARCH

> *Genius is one percent inspiration, ninety-nine percent perspiration.*
> — Thomas Edison (1847-1931)

Discussion

Revisiting the transformational leadership model in light of the perspectives shared by HIIT leaders, by and large participants employ a transformational leadership style. Obtaining and maintaining fitness seems to affect their leadership capacity in positive ways. The fact that these leaders are extreme exercisers provisioned the qualitative examination of physically-fit leaders because their fitness levels are at the higher end of an exercise-intensity range. Developing an operational definition of this continuum could be useful in future quantitative research. Such a continuum could cover a gradient from no exercise at all to extreme exercise, such as performed by HIIT athletes, marathon runners, or tri-athletes. In this study, the research design isolated extreme exercisers, and they tend to be transformational leaders.

Participants serve as role models to their followers (employees), consistent with the idealized influence dimension of transformational leadership. They consider themselves and their employees members of the same team, and will pitch in when needed because they consider goal accomplishment more important than positional authority. They are empathetic to employees, avoiding demands they would see as unreasonable or out of their own reach if their positions were reversed. They strive to buffer employees from organizational concerns that could distract from employees' priorities. They strive to model the passion, focus, discipline, accountability, and achievement that they ask of their employees.

Their perspectives align well with intellectual stimulation also, as they aim to stimulate creativity and innovation. They provide opportunities for growth. They work to create a safe work environment by encouraging exploration and risk-taking, and they find value in failure. They offer flextime to learn new skills, and promote the expansion of paradigms through benchmarking best practices outside their industries.

Participants' behavior is consistent with individual consideration, and in a manner unique to HIIT because they use measurement as a motivational tool. Through measurement, performance is tied to rewards for exceptional performance. They eschew punishment, a transactional leadership behavior, because they know it disengages employees. They hire high-quality employees whom they seek to retain, and see their own success as dependent on the good team members they hire. When employees make mistakes, they regroup, analyze errors, and turn mistakes into continuous improvement opportunities. Val Wright, a leadership consultant who competes in HIIT, offered also: "Leaders are often delusional that underperformers will recognize it in themselves" (as cited by Helm, 2014 para 7). "Meanwhile, the rest of the team wonders why the person isn't being dealt with — and the laggard remains clueless. Identify clear performance standards, let people know when they fall short, and frame it in a way that's geared toward getting the next rep-be it a sales target or a deadline-right the next time" (Helm, 2014, para 7).

The HIIT leaders in this study work to convey an encouraging and moving vision, consistent with inspirational motivation. They devote much energy to developing a clear vision and goals, often collaboratively with teammates. They emphasize team over individual goals, recognize the importance of high standards to spur enthusiasm, and promote employee ownership by maintaining a flexible acknowledgment that many approaches are valid for goal attainment.

The HIIT leaders work in different organizations and industries, so it is difficult to draw conclusions concerning the levels or degrees of stress they face. Lovelace and colleagues (2007) note many stressful components of the general business climate. Leaders must function in conditions of technological change, globalization, scarce resources, higher business costs, downsizing, and demands for flexibility that are inherent to a more contingent workforce. Duties in periods of decline, including baring bad news like employee layoffs, have been associated with headaches, blood-pressure problems, depression, fatigue, burnout, and general feelings of insecurity about one's situation. Positions in this climate are considered stressful because they are demanding, yet mostly outside of the manager's purview (Lovelace et al., 2007). This study did not control for industry or organizational climate; however, all leaders interviewed cope effectively with their environments. In fact, none of the participants offered comments suggesting negative stress or job strain. Rather, the tone they expressed throughout the interviews suggests they derive enjoyment and satisfaction from their work. One proposition is that their fitness enhances effective coping strategies.

Through structural equation modeling, Cartwright and Cooper (2014) found that mental and physical well-being, employee recognition, and happiness predict job satisfaction. They studied employees, not leaders; however, the mind-body dimension of well-being seems salient to this study. When one is healthy, it is reasonable to assume that stress levels are in balance. The experiences common to HIIT and leadership reflect an upbeat mindset, a state of mind supported by their physical health. These leaders experience physical and psychological well-being through achievement and goal attainment. They recruit mental and physical strength as well as a passion that propels them through challenges that they perceive at times as insurmountable in the eyes of many. They are energized by these challenges. Their confidence leaves them open to risk-taking; they are eager for change. They embrace measurement, and remain motivated by continuous feedback and improvement.

Transformational leadership differs from charismatic leadership, although personal charisma is present in both.

"The essence of charisma is being perceived as extraordinary by followers who are dependent on the leader for guidance and inspiration" (Yukl, 2013, p. 329). The influence process is thought to differ between the two models. Yukl explained that transformational leaders inspire and empower followers whereas charismatic leadership "…involves personal identification with an extraordinary leader and dependence on the leader" (p. 329). Although many hold charismatic leaders in high regard, negative charismatic leadership occurs when a leader is elevated in the eyes of followers but abuses this dependence and trust (e.g., Adolph Hitler). Some CrossFit® HIIT critics consider the extreme demands, close communities, and high regard for founder Greg Glassman as cultish (Gregory, 2014). Certainly, HIIT leaders and followers do not routinely reach out to recruit new community members. However, various members joke that they "drank the Kool-Aid," in reference to their initiation. That strong community could make CrossFit® HIIT attractive to negative charismatic leaders, albeit unlikely to be a widespread experience.

Future Research Directions

This exploratory study attempted to fill the research void concerning the mind-body connection as an antecedent to transformational leadership style. The mind is part of the body. The premise of the mind-body connection assumes an association between a healthy body and highly-functioning mental processes necessary for leaders to use social and analytical skills effectively. This research did not prove causation (e.g., one cannot claim that high-intensity exercise "causes" a leader to adopt a transformational style). The results suggest that avid exercisers tend to be transformational leaders. However, qualitative research cannot be generalized beyond the population examined. The emergent themes could provide a foundation for a quantitative survey analysis of constructs. Operational definitions could place constructs like physical fitness, exercise habits, and measures of physical and mental health on a continuum to use as independent variables. Dependent variables could be a host of leadership styles, including transformational and transactional, plus others such as charismatic, laissez-faire, and path-goal. The population could include leaders at all levels of fitness, which would help to better understand the contribution of physical fitness to the overall variance in leadership styles. Employees who report to these leaders could be surveyed to triangulate the data.

Another interesting question is how much exercise is enough to reap benefits. For example, a study could examine whether there is a point of diminishing returns, examining what an optimal exercise level is to achieve the desired effect (walking 40 minutes per day versus running a marathon).

A different question concerns the theme of strategizing and prioritizing as participants anticipate a workout. Participants did not report a parallel between that and strategizing in their leadership roles. However, planning and developing strategies is a useful coping skill to reduce personal stress and to ensure the viability of an organization. Exploring a possible connection between personal and professional strategy formulations could contribute to a deeper understanding. Finally, future research that controls for industry, profession, organizational culture and climate, and levels of stress as antecedents of leadership style could offer a noteworthy contribution.

[9]
CLOSING THOUGHTS

Plans are only good intentions unless they immediately degenerate into hard work.

— Peter Drucker (1909-2005)

Reflecting back on what to take away from this study, the most central message could be expressed as a slogan: "Get fit and stay fit to affect your leadership capacity in a positive way." The study does not suggest a causal connection or statistical correlation because qualitative research cannot supply inferential conclusions. Yet all participants expressed perceived connections.

Leaders are under stress to perform, and must rely on employees to accomplish the goals for which they are responsible. All leaders in this study are successful in their field. Not only do they cope, they also excel. They draw on most all resources available to them, including their mental and physical facilities, to lead effectively. Their physical health is mostly under their control; they are deeply committed to put forth the effort to maintain fitness. The current lifestyle of Juliet in the opening scenario is illustrative. She offered how she needs exercise to facilitate the achievement of her goals:

> *You know sometimes I do not want to go to the gym. I had a hard day and my brain is hurting, my body is aching. It is so much stress. But I know I have to go because I know after I'm done, I'll feel so much better. I'll feel this great sense of relief. I'll feel this tension being tucked away and the only way I found to get rid of this heaviness and this excessive amount of stress that I'm under. Because what I do is very stressful, it is wonderful, it is helping mankind. It is developing wonderful medicines to cure people of diseases but there is a heavy burden with it. There are people dying out there so you've got this heaviness with you, and the stress. And if you don't get it out by exercise you're not going to have enough energy to keep on doing what you need.*

Many people are leaders and managers. Others lead work teams and volunteer organizations. Some are employees who, despite no official position or designation, serve as informal leaders in their work groups. Those wishing to excel further may benefit from integrating exercise into their lives. Transactional leaders focus on rewards and punishment to achieve goal attainment. In contrast, these HIIT leaders use idealized influence, inspirational motivation, intellectual stimulation, and individualized consideration to motivate employees. The risk-benefit ratio clearly favors giving exercise a chance.

Author's Note

Mind-body connections have interested me since childhood. I experienced improved self-confidence, discipline, mental acuity, and well-being whenever I was physically active, and believed that connection was real and worth exploring. My father, now 95 and in excellent health, used to wake me before school or on vacations to run or swim at the start of the day. This was well before running and swimming were widely popular, and a one-mile swim, for example, was normal in my family but unusual at the time. He told me that I needed to "earn" my breakfast. He also taught me that "anything good in life comes through hard work." A correlation between exercise and success through hard work was my belief at a young age because of his parenting. He was a role model because he participated in the exercise alongside me. When I was confirmed at a reformed humanistic synagogue, I gave a talk to the congregation titled, "The moral importance of physical fitness." I realize how difficult beginning an exercise regimen can be for people later in life. However, because physical activity was integrated early, I feel "out of sorts" if I miss even a day of exercise. Exercise taught me self-discipline and confidence, much like the participants in this study.

I started HIIT in my late 40s in 2005. This was my first experience with such high-intensity exercise. The benefits of self-discipline, self-confidence, and sense of accomplishment were familiar, however, the sense of community was something new. Many of my closest friendships were formed through HIIT.

I am a program coordinator at Siena Heights University, where I mentor part-time faculty in addition to teaching management and leadership courses. Since studying management, I have embraced the transformational leadership model. I always desired to report to a transformational leader as an employee; similarly, I attempt to apply its tenants to my own leadership.

As a HIIT athlete, I brought bias into the study. I expected to find a correlation between high-intensity exercise and transformational leadership. However, I was careful to follow a research protocol that was designed to minimize my bias. The research protocol measured both transformational and transactional leadership styles. The Delphi technique provided the participants an opportunity to comment on the data, and to reach a consensus on the data analysis. I used a constant protocol in transcribing and coding the data, and creating nodes, and subsequently themes from the nodes. I used member checking to verify the accuracy of the transcripts and themes. I recognize this study is a starting point, and hope that I and others will conduct further research to advance this agenda.

[10]

Author's Suggested Readings & References

We ask the authors of our mini-monographs to provide a minimum of three titles of supplementary materials they consider essential reading pertaining to the subject they wrote about. It is hoped that the mini-monograph you just read will have sparked your curiosity and interest for further study.

Dr. Himelhoch suggests these titles:

Suggested Reading

Dossey, L. (1999). *Reinventing medicine: Beyond mind-body to a new era of healing.* San Francisco: Harper San Francisco.

Pearce, C. L. (2007). The future of leadership development: The importance of identity, multi-level approaches, self-leadership, physical fitness, shared leadership, networking, creativity, emotions, spirituality, and on-boarding processes. *Human Resource Management Review, 17*(4), 355-359.

Tabrizi, B. & Terrell, M. (2013). *The inside out effect: A practical guide to transformational leadership.* Ashland, OH: Evolve Publishing, Inc.

Essential Reading

Bass, B. M. (1996). *A new paradigm for leadership: An inquiry into transformational leadership.* Alexandria, VA: U.S. Army Research Institute for the Behavioral and Social Sciences.

Goleman, D., Boyatzis, R. E., & McKee, A. (2002). *The new leaders: Transforming the art of leadership into the science of results.* London: Little, Brown.

Yukl, G. (1989). Managerial leadership: A review of theory and research. *Journal of Management, 15*(2), 251-289.

List of References

Amon, G., (2014). Type D personality and job burnout: The moderating role of physical activity. *Personality and Individual Differences, 58*, 112-115.

Atwater, L.E. & Yammarino, F.J. (1993). Personal attributes as predictors of superiors' and subordinates' perceptions of military academy leadership. *Human Relations, 46*, 645-668.

Babbie, E. R. (2010). *The practice of social research* (12th ed.). Belmont, CA: Wadsworth.

Baker, J., Lovell, K., & Harris, N. (2006). How expert are the experts? An exploration of the concept of 'expert' within Delphi panel techniques. *Nurse Researcher, 14*(1), 59-70.

Barling, J., Christie, A.M., & Hoption, C. (2011). Leadership. In S. Zedeck (Ed.), *APA handbook of industrial and organizational psychology* (Vol. 1). Washington, DC: American Psychological Association.

Barling, J., Lys, R., Bergenwall, A., Byren, A., Dioniski, A., Dupre, K., Robertson, J., & Wylie, J. (2012). *Being well, leading well? Leaders' psychological distress predicts leadership behaviors.* Paper presented at The University of Michigan, Interdisciplinary Committee on Organizational Studies on March, 23rd, Ann Arbor, MI.

Bass, B. M. (1985). *Leadership and performance beyond expectations.* New York: Free Press.

Bono, J.E. & Judge, T.A. (2004). Personality and transformational and transactional leadership: A meta-analysis. *Journal of Applied Psychology, 89*, 901-910.

Burns, J.M. (1978). *Leadership.* NY: Harper and Row.

Boyzatis, R.E., Smith, M.L., & Blase, N. (2006). Developing sustainable leaders through coaching and passion. *Academy of Management Learning & Education, 5*(1), 8-24.

Cartwright, S., & Cooper, C. L. (2014). Towards organizational health: Stress, positive organizational behavior, and employee well-being. In G.F. Bauer & O. Hämmig (Eds.), *Bridging Occupational, Organizational and Public Health* (pp. 29-42). Dordrecht, Netherlands: Springer.

Çelik, D. A. (2014). *Leadership re-defined: A whole soul model for the global and diverse work contexts.* Retrieved from Inter-Disciplinary.net: http://www.inter-disciplinary.net/

Church, T. (2014). Exercise and weight management. In G.A. Bray & C. Bouchard (Eds.), *Handbook of obesity: Epidemiology, etiology, and physiopathology (3rd ed.)* (p. 207-218). Boca Raton, FL: CRC Press.

Colditz, G.A., & Bohlke, K. (2014). Priorities for the primary prevention of breast cancer. *CA:A Cancer Journal for Clinicians, 64*(3), 186-194.

Colton, D., & Covert, R.W. (2007). *Designing and constructing instruments for social research and evaluation* (1st ed.). San Francisco, CA: Jossey-Bass.

Creswell, J. W. (2009). *Research design: Qualitative, quantitative, and mixed methods approaches* (3rd ed.). Thousand Oaks, CA: Sage Publishing, Inc.

Cross, R., Baker, W., & Parker, A. (2003, July). What creates energy in organizations? *MIT Sloan Management Review.* Retrieved from http://sloanreview.mit.edu

Douw L, Nieboer D., van Dijk B.W., Stam C.J., Twisk J.W. (2014) A healthy brain in a healthy body: Brain network correlates of physical and mental fitness. *PLoS ONE* 9(2): e88202. doi:10.1371/journal.pone.0088202.

Du Plessis, E., & Human, S. (2007). The art of the Delphi technique: Highlighting its scientific merit. *Health SA Gesondheid*, *12*(4), 13-24.

Gerdes, D.A., (2001). Leadership education: Physical activity and the affective domain. *Physical Educator, 58*(2), p. 78.

Gibala, M.J., Little, J.P., MacDonald, M.J., & Hawley, J.A. (2012). Physiological adaptations to low-volume, high-intensity interval training in health and disease. *The Journal of Physiology, 590*, 1077-1084.

Gregory, S. (2014, January). Five things to know about CrossFit. *Time Magazine*. Retrieved from http://nation.time.com/2014/01/10/five-things-you-need-to-know-about-crossfit/.

Halling, S. (2008). *Intimacy, transcendence, and psychology*. New York, NY: Palgrave MacMillan.

Heaphy, E.D. & Dutton, J. E. (2008). Positive social interactions and the human body at work: Linking organizations and physiology. *Academy of Management Review, 33*, 137-162.

Helm, B. (2014, February). What CrossFit can teach you about leadership. *Inc.* Retrieved from http://www.inc.com/burt-helm/what-crossfit-taught-me-about-leadership.html.

Heyman, E. (2010). *Overcoming student retention issues in higher education online programs: A Delphi study.* (Doctoral dissertation). Retrieved from ProQuest Dissertations & Theses Database. (Publication No. AAT 3417611.)

Iqbal, S. & Pipon-Young, L. (2009). The Delphi method. *Psychologist, 22*(7), 598-600.

Juniper, B. (2011). Defining wellbeing. *Occupational Health, 63*(10), p. 25.

Jonsdottir, I. H., Gerber, M., Lindwall, M., Lindegård, A., & Börjesson, M. (2013). The role of physical activity and fitness in prevention and treatment of mental health. *Proceedings of the International Journal of Exercise Science, 10*(1), (p. 72).

Lasikiewicz, N., Myrissa, K., Hoyland, A., & Lawton, C.L. (2014). Psychological benefits of weight loss following behavioural and/or dietary weight loss interventions. A systematic research review. *Appetite, 72*(1), 123-137.

Lewis, M., & Staehler, T. (2010). *Phenomenology: An introduction*. New York, NY: Continuum International Publishing Group.

Littrell, J. (2008). The mind-body connection. *Social Work in Health Care, 46*(4), 17-37.

Lovelace, K.J., Manz, C.C., & Alves, J.C. (2007). Work stress and leadership development: The role of self-leadership, shared leadership, physical fitness and flow in managing demands and increasing job control. *Human Resource Management Review, 17*, 347-387.

Luckhaupt, S.E.; Cohen, M.A.; Li, J.; & Calvert, G.M. (2014). Prevalence of obesity among U.S. workers and associations with occupational factors. *American Journal of Preventative Medicine, 46*(3), 237-248.

Makris, A., Lent, R., & Foster, G.D. (2014). Diet composition and weight loss. In G.A. Bray & C. Bouchard (Eds.), *Handbook of obesity: Epidemiology, etiology, and physiopathology (3rd ed.)* (p. 177-192). Boca Raton, FL: CRC Press

Meadows, C. (2013). *Mind body therapies*. Retrieved from The University of Minnesota's Center for Spirituality and Healing: http://www.takingcharge.csh.umn.edu/explore-healing-practices/what-are-mind-body-therapies.

Mitra, A. (2014). Flexibility, controllability and risk measurement metrics in changing pattern of business environment. In Sushil & E.A. Stohr (Eds.), *The flexible enterprise* (pp. 173-196). New Delhi, India: Springer

Nanjundeswaras, T.S., & Swamy, D.R. (2014). Leadership styles. *Advances in Management, 7*(2), 57-62.

Neck, C.P., & Cooper, K.H. (2000). The fit executive: Exercise and diet guidelines for enhancing performance. *The Academy of Management Executive, 14*(2), 72-83.

Pally, R. (1998). Emotional processing: The mind-body connection. *The International Journal of Psychoanalysis 79*(2), 349-362.

Pflanz, S.E., & Ogle, A.D. (2006). Job stress, depression, work performance, and perceptions of supervisors in military personnel. *Military Medicine, 171*(9), 861-865.

Privitera, G.J., Antonelli, D.E., & Szal, A.L. (2014). An enjoyable distraction during exercise augments positive effects of exercise on mood. *Journal of Sports Science and Medicine, 13*, 266-270.

Robertson, I.T., & Cooper, C.L., (2010). Full engagement: The integration of employee engagement and psychological well-being. *Leadership and Organizational Development Journal, 31*(4), 324-336.

Sarno, J.E. (1991). *Healing back pain*. New York: Hachette Book Group.

Schippers, M.C. & Hogenes, R. (2011). Energy management of people in organizations: A review and research agenda. *Journal of Business and Psychology, 26*(2), 193-203.

Seidell, J.C. (2014). Worldwide prevalence of obesity in adults. In G.A. Bray & C. Bouchard (Eds.), *Handbook of obesity: Epidemiology, etiology, and physiopathology (3rd ed.)* (p. 47-54). Handbook of obesity: Epidemiology, etiology, and physiopathology. Boca Raton, FL: CRC Press

Seimon, R. V., Espinoza, D., Ivers, L., Gebski, V., Finer, N., Legler, U. F., … Caterson, I. D. (2014). Changes in body weight and blood pressure: paradoxical outcome events in overweight and obese subjects with cardio-vascular disease. *International Journal of Obesity*. doi:10.1038/ijo.2014.2

Skulmoski, G. J., Hartman, F. T., & Krahn, J. (2007). The Delphi method for graduate research. *Journal of Information Technology Education, 6*(1), 1-21.

Seligman, M.P., Steen, T.A., Park, N. & Petersen, C. (2005). Positive psychology progress: Empirical validation of interventions. *American Psychologist, 60*(5), 410-421.

Smith, J. A., Flowers, P., & Larkin, M. (2009). *Interpretative phenomenological analysis*. Thousand Oaks, CA: Sage Publications Inc.

Thompson, W.R. (2013). Now trending: Worldwide survey of fitness trends for 2014. *ACSM'S Health & Fitness Journal, 17*(6), 10-20.

Verhoef, M. J., & White, M. A. (2002). Factors in making the decision to forgo conventional cancer treatment. *Cancer Practice, 10*(4), 201–207. doi:10.1046/j.1523-5394.2002.104002.x

Walter, F., & Bruch, H. (2009). An affective events model of charismatic leadership behavior: A review, theoretical integration, and research agenda. *Journal of Management, 35*(6), 1428-1452.

Warrick, D.D. (2011). The urgent need for skilled transformational leaders: Integrating transformational leadership and organizational development. *Journal of Leadership, Accountability, and Ethics, 8*(5), 11-26.

Westerteterp-Plantenga, M.S. (2014). Dietary protein and weight management. In G.A. Bray & C. Bouchard (Eds.), *Handbook of obesity: Epidemiology, etiology, and physiopathology (3rd ed.)* (p. 193-206). Handbook of obesity: Epidemiology, etiology, and physiopathology. Boca Raton, FL: CRC Press

Woo, S.E., Chernyshenko, O.S., Stark, S.E., & Conz, G. (2014). Validity of six openness facets in predicting work behaviors: A meta-analysis. *Journal of Personality Assessment, 96*(1), 76-86.

Yukl, G. (2013). *Leadership in organizations* (8th ed.). New York, NY: Prentice Hall.

Additional Bibliography of Interest

Bass, B. M. (1990). *Handbook of leadership: A survey of theory and research.* New York: Free Press.

Bass B. M. & Avolio B. J. (1990). Developing transformational leadership: 1992 and beyond. *Journal of European Industrial Training, 14,* 21–27.

Caillier, J. G. (2014). Linking transformational leadership to self-efficacy, extra-role behaviors, and turnover intentions in public agencies: The mediating role of goal clarity. *Administration & Society,* doi: 10.1177 /0095 399713519093

Fischer, R. (1978). The Delphi method: A description, review, and criticism. *Journal of Academic Librarianship, 4*(2), 64-70.

Fredrickson, B.L. (1998). What good are positive emotions? *Review of General Psychology, 2*(4), 300-19.

Fredrickson, B.L. & Joiner, T. (2002), Positive emotions trigger upward spirals toward emotional well-being. *Psychological Science, 13*(2), 172-175.

Hambrick, D.C., Finkelstein, S., & Mooney, A.C. (2005). Executive job demands: New insights for explaining strategic decisions and leader behaviors. *Academy of Management Review, 30*(30), 472-491.

Hoffman, D. M. (2009). Multiple methods, communicative preferences and the incremental interview approach protocol. Forum: *Qualitative social research, 10*(1), 1-19.

Kerfoot, K. M. (2007). Leadership, civility, and the 'no jerks' rule. *Nursing Economics, 25*(4), 233-4, 227.

Leedy, P. D., & Ormrod, J. E. (2010). *Practical research: Planning and design* (9th ed.). Upper Saddle River, NJ: Merrill Prentice Hall.

Ly, R. (2009). *Future direction for information technology professionals: A Delphi study of industry trends and direction* (Doctoral dissertation). Retrieved from ProQuest Dissertations and Theses database. (UMI No. 3381826).

McDermott, R. (2008). Presidential leadership, illness, and decision making. *Choice Reviews Online*, 45(12), 45-7059-45-7059. doi:10.5860/CHOICE.45-7059

McDowell-Larsen, S., Kearney, L., & Campbell, D. (2002). Fitness and leadership: Is there a relationship? Regular exercise correlates with higher leadership ratings in senior-level executives. *Journal of Managerial Psychology, 17*(4), 316-324.

Miller, D. C., & Salkind, N. J. (2002). *Handbook of research design and social measurement* (6th ed.). Thousand Oaks: Sage Publishing, Inc.

Morse, J., Stern, P. N., Corbin, J., Bowers, B., Charmaz, K., & Clarke, A. (2009). *Developing grounded theory: The second generation*. Walnut Creek, CA: Left Coast Press, Inc.

Ryan, M. (2009). Making visible the coding process: Using qualitative data software in a post-structural study. *Issues in Educational Research, 19*(2), 142-161.

Sutton, R. (2007). *The no asshole rule*. New York: Warner Business Books.

[11]
APPENDIX A

Interview Protocol

Thank you very much for participating in my study. It's a study in leadership. The ways that the lived experiences of avid exercisers intersect with leadership styles has never been examined before so this is kind of an exploratory study. I'm conducting interviews with a few people to try to get a sense of what that experience is like, and I've asked you, particularly, because your profile is of somebody who is an avid exerciser, and you serve as a leader in your career. I have a series of 20 questions.

1. How did you get involved with [high-intensity interval training]?

   • How did you develop an interest/passion for such high-intensity exercise?

2. In what ways has [HIIT] changed you?

3. How do you feel about yourself as a [HIIT] athlete, so to speak? How does your high-intensity training influence the way you think about yourself, your identity, your outlook?

4. What does it mean to you to be a high-intensity athlete?

5. What's it like for you when you go to the gym?

6. How do you interact with other people during the workout? How do you feel about those interactions?

7. How do you feel before, during, and after a workout?

8. Think back to before you started doing high-intensity workouts. How do you think they have changed your outlook on life?

9. Let's shift into a new topic - leadership. How do you deal with people in your role as a leader?

10. In what ways do you serve as a role model?

11. To what extent do you establish a vision that encourages and inspires your subordinates?

12. How important is a clear chain of command to you as a leader? (transactional)

13. Can you explain how you use rewards and punishment in your leadership role? (transactional)

14. How do you coach, support, and encourage your subordinates?

15. How do you stimulate your subordinates to be innovative and creative?

16. How do you monitor your subordinates to ensure that they are meeting your expectations? (transactional)

17. Given all of this, how do you feel about your relationships with your subordinates?

18. How would your subordinates describe you as a leader?

Let's shift gears again. We've talked about some of your reactions and thoughts about [HIIT] and exercise and what it means to you. We've also talked about some issues surrounding your leadership. Now let's explore some of the connections you think there might be.

19. What do you think, maybe consciously or unconsciously, the connections are between your life as a high-intensity athlete and what you do as a leader?

20. How has your leadership influenced your [HIIT] experience?

21. Is there anything else I haven't mentioned?

[12]

Afterword

MindBodyMed Press's Manuscript Review

Introduction

The Eight-Fold Path to a Publishable Mini-Monograph

All manuscripts received are reviewed by the managing editor based on MindBodyMed Press's "Eight-Fold Path to a Publishable Mini-Monograph."

This evaluation process allows us to appraise all manuscripts we receive based on the same basic quality guidelines. Once a manuscript passes all eight checkpoints, we believe that we have a high-quality mini-monograph on our hands. Such a mini-monograph has the potential to add additional quality information to the field of CAM and mind-body medicine, filling a void that currently exists in the way sharing of scientific information occurs with the public.

A brief overview of our evaluation criteria, along with an explanation of each item, follows.

1. Quality of design and methods
2. Clarity and readability
3. Literature review and use of references
4. Adequate data analyses
5. Rationale and theoretical development of hypotheses
6. Legitimacy of conclusions
7. Quality of discussion
8. Contributes new knowledge in the field

1. Quality of Design and Methods

Good guidelines exist for almost any type of research. The design and methods will vary with type of study. We want to know if reporting in the mini-monograph is based on generally accepted methods of scientific research in the field the author engages in. This will give a picture of reliability and validity of the reporting in the mini-monograph (American Psychological Association, 2010).

2. Clarity and Readability

Here, we look for whether the manuscript is the optimal length to allow the author to communicate effectively the primary ideas elaborated on in the mini-monograph. Does the structure of the mini-monograph help develop the argument? Are headings and paragraphs, lists, tables, numbering used appropriately? Are ideas presented so they can be followed easily? How about smoothness of expression? Does the text flow easily and effortlessly? Is the author's tone appropriate for the manuscript? Is the author communicating with precision and clarity? Does the author avoid bias? Does the author communicate with an educated lay audience in mind (American Psychological Association, 2010)?

3. Literature Review and Use of References

A literature review discusses written knowledge in a distinct subject area. A literature review may be only a mere summary of the references, but it customarily has an organizational pattern and consolidates both summary and synthesis. A summary is a recap of the essential knowledge of the source, but a synthesis is a re-organization of that information. It might provide a brand-new appreciation of old material or blend new with old themes. A literature review might ascertain the intellectual progress of the field, covering major debates (University of North Carolina, n.d.).

The literature review may assess the sources and inform the reader on the most appropriate or applicable sources pertaining a subject area. In a research paper, one applies the literature as a basis and support for a novel idea that the author has (University of North Carolina, n.d.).

For research falling into the realm of quantitative literature reviews and research papers employing a quantitative methodology, we evaluate literature reviews based on The PRISMA Statement: The Preferred Reporting System for Systematic Reviews and Meta-Analyses (Liberati et al., 2009).

For a study, that involves mainly qualitative research, we evaluate the literature reviews based on Noblit and Hare (1998), Ogawa and Malen (1992) and Gall, Borg and Gall (1996). Evaluating literature reviews for phenomenological studies we look for guidance to Moustakas (1994).

Boote and Beile's (2005) Literature Review Scoring Rubric highlights key points we seek out in a literature review, regardless of the investigation's methodology.

We also want to know whether the author cites relevant material. Do those citations provide enough background information to support the author's hypothesis? Do the citations place the author's contribution to the field in the context? Is each key point supported with a minimum of one or two sources that are most representative of that key point (American Psychological Association, 2010)?

4. Adequate Data Analyses

The next item we assess is whether or not the author's data analyses make sense. We want to know that the author bases the conclusions on adequate data analyses or evaluation of the data. For a very interesting discussion on the term "statistical significance" see Field (2009). In this discussion, Field (2009) mentions an article by Fisher (1956) in which Fisher acknowledged that:

> *No scientific worker has a fixed level of significance at which from year to year, and in all circumstances, he rejects hypotheses; he rather gives his mind to each particular case in the light of the evidence and his ideas. (Fisher, 1956, as cited by Field, 2009, p. 51)*

In other words, "statistically significant" is an arbitrary entity and the magic $p < 0.05$ or $p < 0.01$ are popular trends to report test statistics as being significant at these levels. The most simplistic answer probably is that, during the days before computers, scientists compared their test statistics against published tables of "critical values." It so happened that Fisher, to save space in his far reaching textbook "Statistical methods for research workers" produced only tables for probability values of 0.05, 0.02, and 0.01. So, for no reason other than being readily available, these values encroached themselves on modern statistics as the "gold standard" to report statistically significant results.

The very focus of many peer-review journals on statistical significance might contribute to the file drawer problem or, in other words, reporting bias. This means that research that could inform the field and might be pretty important to move the field ahead – because of the ideas contained – will not get published because the results do not show statistical significance. The Cochrane Collaboration writes that publication biases arise when statistically positive results are being "more likely to be published," "more likely to be published rapidly," "more likely to be published in English," "more likely to be published more than once," and "more likely to be cited by others" (Higgins & Green, 2011).

The take home message here is to know that publication bias exists. Here at MindBodyMed Press we focus on the publication of mini-monographs based on sound scientific principles, regardless whether or not statistically significant results are being reported (where applicable).

5. Rationale and Theoretical Development of Hypotheses

Does the author introduce a problem and is it supported by background material? Does the author state the hypothesis or specific question? Is the hypothesis or specific question clearly derivable from theory and/or logically connected to earlier data and arguments? Does the author explain how a particular research design allows the extra-polations needed to scrutinize the hypothesis or the specific question (American Psychological Association, 2010)?

6. Legitimacy of Conclusions

Is the data summarized and adequately analyzed? Is there enough data and in sufficient detail to support the author's conclusion? Did the author attempt to elaborate on all results, even those that were unexpected (American Psychological Association, 2010)?

7. Quality of Discussion

Does the author make, if appropriate, a declarative, and concise assertion of the study results? Does the author elaborate on the meaning of research results and state why these findings are important? Did the author relate findings to similar studies that inspired the author's investigation in the first place? Does the author consider ALL possible explanations rather than only those that fit the author's own biases (Hess, 2004)?

Most importantly, does the author address patients and clinicians by providing at least some context of the findings for the care of patients? Does the author provide some context of the findings for other researchers and to provide suggestions for further study? How about the limitations of the investigation? Simply stated, all studies have limitations, and it is the responsibility of the researcher to point out those limitations and delimitations. Conversely, does the author mention the strengths of the investigation (Hess, 2004)?

8. Conclusion: Contributes New Knowledge to the Field

Here, we look at the "Take-Home Message" of the study. It is essentially an opportunity for the author to elaborate and highlight important points a reader should remember from this mini-monograph (Hess, 2004). The conclusion section also provides an opportunity to provide suggestions for change, if appropriate.

Hess (2004) writes that one should avoid inflating the interpretation of the results, making unwarranted speculations and overly inflating the importance of the findings. It is imperative to stay concentrated on the results, rather than weakening and muddling the real message of the study with tangential hyperbole. Finally, Hess suggests abstaining from using the discussion section to flat-out attack other researchers or "preaching" to the reader and providing conclusions not supported by the data.

Overall Impact and Criterion Scoring

Now that the reader has an idea about **WHAT** we evaluate and analyze when appraising a mini-monograph proposal, it is equally necessary to have an objective rating scheme to evaluate the territory of the eight-fold path network (overall score) as well as the terrain of each distinct path (criterion score)- the **HOW**.

While many methods and schemes exist to evaluate manuscripts, we borrowed and modified a scoring system used by the National Institutes of Health (NIH) to evaluate grant proposals. For the NIH's system, see the document titled "Scoring System and Procedure" (NIH, 2013).

How Dœs MindBodyMed Press's Scoring System Work?

Overall Impact Score

The overall impact score indicates an appraisal of a project to have a sustained, significant importance on the research fields affected. Reviewers base impact scores on the appraisal of the scored criteria as well as additional criteria. A score can range from one to nine. The score is next multiplied by 10 to decide the final impact score. Thus, the final range of one unique overall impact score for a mini-monograph manuscript is 10 to 90.

Criterion Scoring

The purpose of criterion scoring is to communicate the reviewer's assessment of strengths and weaknesses of individual sections. For criterion scoring, the reviewer gives a score of one to nine along with a written summary critique for each criterion. It must be pointed out that the overall impact score is not the average of the criterion scores.

Reviewer Guidance

The NIH (2013) scoring system and procedure document provides reviewer direction. This material also comprises a table of a score's meaning and description.

Each criterion score, however, should be imposed based on the strength of that particular criterion in the context of the manuscript. It is possible for a reviewer to give only moderate scores to part of the review criteria, yet still give a high overall impact score. This is conceivable because a single review criterion critically vital to the research could be rated high, despite moderate scores being assigned elsewhere, thus giving the whole project a higher impact score (NIH, 2013).

On the other hand, a reviewer might give chiefly high criterion ratings, but rate the overall impact score low, because one criterion critically important to the mini-monograph is not highly rated. The NIH accepts the idea that not all grant applications can or need to be strong in each and every of the evaluation criteria to be still regarded as having excellent overall impact. If this evaluation process is good enough for the NIH (with a 2014 budget of $29.9 billion), it most assuredly merits adoption by an emerging indie publisher such as MindBodyMed Press.

See Table 2 "Guide for Reviewers Assigning Overall Impact Scores and Individual Criterion Scores" on the next page.

While it may be to some extent counterintuitive, the lower the score the better the manuscript. For instance, an overall impact score of 5 is representative of a good, medium-impact mini-monograph.

We must acknowledge that this method is by no means complete or fail safe as a reviewer's personal biases still may find their way into the evaluation process. In spite of that, this process renders a framework that permits individual manuscripts to be appraised based on objective criteria omitting reviewer bias to some degree.

This, in a nutshell, is our evaluation method. Since

each manuscript is different, not all forks of the "Eight-Fold Path to a Publishable Mini-Monograph" apply uniformly to all evaluations.

If you are an author thinking about submitting a manuscript, you now have a simple checklist to examine your manuscript as you tailor your document toward publication with MindBodyMed Press.

On the other hand, if you are a consumer reading this, you can rest assured that we have taken multiple precautions to report only important, high-quality material, without the hype the latest treatment, miracle cure, and magic pill usually receive and that plaque the field of Complementary and Alternative Medicine.

Thus, MindBodyMed Press pursues its vision of empowering doctors, CAM practitioners, mind-body practitioners, clinicians, and scientists, who are the key holders

■ Table 2. Guide for Reviewers Assigning Overall Impact Scores and Individual Criterion Scores		
Overall Impact or Criterion Strength	Score	Descriptor
High	1	Exceptional
High	2	Outstanding
High	3	Excellent
Medium	4	Very Good
Medium	5	Good
Medium	6	Satisfactory
Low	7	Fair
Low	8	Marginal
Low	9	Poor
Note. Adapted from "Scoring System and Procedure" by the National Institutes of Health, 2013, p. 4. Copyright by the National Institutes of Health.		

of knowledge associated with the potential use of mind-body interventions, to provide and share information that is of value to the public.

We believe that making the evaluation process transparent adds value to our mini-monographs and therefore have included the reviewer's comments in the afterword.

Adding transparency to these steps, even though we are not a peer-review journal per se, further positions MindBodyMed Press as a leader in changing the way mind-body scientists, clinicians, and practitioners communicate with the public.

Werner Absenger
Managing Editor and Publisher MindBodyMed Press
werner@MindBodyMedPress.com

References:

American Psychological Association. (2010). *Publication Manual of the American Psychological Association* (6th ed.). Washington, DC: American Psychological Association.

Field, A. (2009). *Discovering statistics using SPSS: (And sex and drugs and rock "n" roll)* (3rd ed.). London: SAGE.

Gall, M. D., Borg, W. R., & Gall, J. P. (1996). *Education research: An introduction* (6th ed.). White Plains, NY: Longman.

Hess, D. R. (2004). How to write an effective discussion. *Respiratory Care*, 49(10), 1238–41.

Higgins, J. P., & Green, S. (Eds.). (2011). *Cochrane handbook for systematic reviews of interventions version 5.1.0* [updated March 2011]. The Cochrane Collaboration. Retrieved from www.cochrane-handbook.org

Liberati, A., Altman, D. G., Tetzlaff, J., Mulrow, C., Gotzsche, P. C., Ioannidis, J. P. A., … Moher, D. (2009). The PRISMA statement for reporting systematic reviews and meta-analyses of studies that evaluate healthcare interventions: Explanation and elaboration. *BMJ*, 339, b2700–b2700. doi:10.1136/bmj.b2700

Moustakas, C. (1994). *Phenomenological research methods.* Thousand Oaks, CA: Sage.

National Institutes of Health. (2013, March 25). *Scoring system and procedure.* Retrieved from National Institutes of Health (NIH) website: http://grants.nih.gov/grants/-peer/guidelines_general/scoring_system_and_procedure.pdf

Noblit, G. W., & Hare, R. D., (1988). *Meta-ethnography: Synthesizing qualitative studies.* Newbury Park, CA: Sage.

Ogawa, R. T. & Malen, B. (1991). Towards rigor in reviews of multivocal literature: Applying the exploratory case method. *Review of Educational Research*, 61, 265-286.

University of North Carolina. (n.d.). *Literature reviews.* Retrieved from website: https://writingcenter.unc.edu/-handouts/literature reviews/

[12]

AFTERWORD: MANUSCRIPT REVIEW

Carol R. Himelhoch: Transformational Leadership and High-Intensity Interval Training

Evaluated by Werner Absenger on April 26, 2014

1. Quality of Design and Methods:

Comments:

Dr. Himelhoch explicitly declares her research question in Chapter 2. She distinctly describes the study population as well as her research process which is "…an interpretative phenomenological analysis with a modified Delphi technique…" (p. 16). The Delphi method was first developed by RAND Corporation in the 1950s. The core of the method is that a group of experts responds to a questionnaire. These experts receive feedback from the researcher concerning the initial "group response." This process repeats itself with the aim to decrease the range of responses in order to reach an expert consensus (RAND Corporation, 2014). Dr. Himelhoch's selection of the research question and methodology are highly suitable to inquire into the relationship between physical fitness and adoption of transformational leadership style by managers engaging in a HIIT regimen.

Criterion Score: 1 (High): Exceptional

(2014). Delphi Method. Retrieved (June 8, 2014) from the RAND Corporation website: http://www.rand.org/topics/delphi-method.html

2. Clarity and Readability:

Comments:

Dr. Himelhoch's manuscript is of an excellent length to express her ideas persuasively. The manuscript has a very good structure with exceptional use of chapters, figures, and a table. Headings are designed to enable the reader to easily grasp the argument set forth in this mini-monograph. Dr. Himelhoch's voice and smoothness of expression add clarity and allow the text to flow smooth and effortlessly. She dodges bias wherever likely, but points out in the manuscript that, as a HIIT athlete herself, she brings bias to the study. Nevertheless, her research is designed to lessen the bias she brings to this study. Dr. Himelhoch has written the manuscript with an educated lay audience in mind.

Criterion Score: 2 (High): Outstanding

3. Literature Review and Use of References:

Comments:

Dr. Himelhoch did not discuss a specific method applied for her literature review. What follows are comments based on a paper titled "Methods for the synthesis of qualitative research: a critical review" (Barnett-Page & Thomas, 2009) and Boote and Beile's Literature Review Scoring Rubric (Boote & Beile, 2005).

Dr. Himelhoch's literature review fits the model of "Lines-of-argument (LOA) synthesis…" (Barnett-Page & Thomas, 2009, p.59), to construct a picture of the whole with the studies she cites. It appears that Dr. Himelhoch provides a very brief synthesis of the literature mentioned. The brief "narrative" synthesis and her summary of the written knowledge in the field she investigates are enough to substantiate her research design and method. I would have liked to have seen more in depth critique of the literature, which would have allowed Dr. Himelhoch to offer a new perspective, while also aiding in substantiating the need for her research even more.

Literature Review Coverage

According to Boote and Beile (2005), a researcher should strive to justify inclusion and exclusion criteria for including literature into a literature review. Dr. Himelhoch did not discuss criteria for inclusion and exclusion of the literature for her review. However, the idea of her literature review was slightly different than to compose a free-standing literature review.

While Dr. Himelhoch discussed what has and has not been done in the field, she did not critically examine the state of the field. Her discussion of the field, though, is sufficient to put her research project into the setting.

Dr. Himelhoch did a very good job in reviewing relationships amongst her key variables and phenomena.

Literature Review Significance

Dr. Himelhoch's literature review provides the reader with a brief analysis and rationalization of the practical as well as the scholarly importance of the research problem. I would have liked to have Dr. Himelhoch critique both the practical as well as the scholarly significance of the research to further substantiate her own research.

Literature Review Rhetoric.

Dr. Himelhoch's literature review is composed in a coherent, clear structure that underpins the review.

I must point out again that the criteria set forth by Boote and Beile (2005) and Barnett-Page and Thomas (2009) are for full-fledged literature reviews meant to serve as stand alone, publishable research. Thus, adopting all the requirements for such a literature review to substantiate the ideas presented within a mini-monograph is superfluous and unnecessary. However, these guidelines provide an ideal structure to evaluate literature reviews within mini-monographs such as the one presented by Dr. Himelhoch. Based on this evaluation, Dr. Himelhoch did a very good job acquainting the reader to the most relevant and applicable sources pertaining to the subject area.

Criterion Score: 4 (Medium): Good

References:

Barnett-Page, E., & Thomas, J. (2009). Methods for the synthesis of qualitative research: A critical review. *BMC Medical Research Methodology, 9*(1), 59. doi:10.1186/1471-2288-9-59

Boote, D. N., & Beile, P. (2005). Scholars before researchers: On the centrality of the dissertation literature review in research preparation. *Educational Researcher, 34*(6), 3–15. doi:10.3102/0013189X034006003

4. Adequate Data Analyses:

Comments:

Dr. Himelhoch's research design permitted her to draw meaningful conclusions pertaining to the transformational leadership style and the HIIT experience. In the manuscript, she explains what can and cannot be measured by her study design. She presents validity and reliability of her research design. The emerging themes are clearly stated and elaborated on, as well as highlighted by, the suitable use of figures.

Criterion Score: 1 (High): Exceptional

5. Rationale and Theoretical Development of Hypotheses:

Comments:

Dr. Himelhoch introduces the problem very early on. She then substantiates the problem with a very good literature review. She clearly states the research questions. Dr. Himelhoch clearly explains how her chosen research design allows her to extrapolate the data in order to scrutinize her specific research question.

Criterion Score: 2 (High): Outstanding

6. Legitimacy of Conclusions:

Comments:

With the use of figures, Dr. Himelhoch summarizes the data exceptionally well. Her data seems adequately analyzed and supported by clear language pertaining to emerging themes. Her interviews provide very rich content, drilled down into sufficient detail to support Dr. Himelhoch's conclusions. Dr. Himelhoch provides commentary on all of her results.

Criterion Score: 1 (High): Exceptional

7. Quality of Discussion:

Comments:

Dr. Himelhoch provides an excellent discussion section. She elaborates on and makes concise assertions of her study results. Dr. Himelhoch elucidates the meaning of the research results and provides an explanation on why these findings are important. In the discussion section, Dr. Himelhoch takes the opportunity to relate findings to similar studies. She provides context for other researchers as well as the general public.

The only shortcoming of Dr. Himelhoch's discussion section is that she could have elaborated more on the weaknesses of her research. Dr. Himelhoch also did not spend enough time developing the strengths of her study.

Criterion Score: 2 (High): Outstanding

8. Contributes to New Knowledge in the Field:

Comments:

Without inflating the interpretation of her results, Dr. Himelhoch provides segue for further research. The "take-home" message of her study is clearly articulated. She also provides several examples of what type of research might move the field forward.

Criterion Score: 2 (High): Outstanding

Overall Mini-Monograph Impact Score and Comments:

Comments:

Dr. Himelhoch's mini-monograph on "Transformational Leadership and High-Intensity Interval Training" is an account of five HIIT athletes and managers from diverse industries.

Dr. Himelhoch's study is exceptionally well crafted and skillfully organized. She uses the mini-monograph to draw us closer to the experiences of managers who also relish the life of high-intensity athletes and the consequence of such a lifestyle on managerial leadership behavior.

Her study is very well conceived and executed very well adhering to established norms in phenomenological research. Dr. Himelhoch's election of the research question and methodology are highly suitable to make an inquiry into the relationship between physical fitness and adoption of transformational leadership style by managers engaging in a HIIT regimen.

The manuscript has a particularly solid structure with outstanding use of chapters, figures, and a table. Headings are sketched to enable the reader to quickly follow the argument set forth in this mini-monograph. Dr. Himelhoch's voice and smoothness of expression add clarity and allow the text to flow smooth and effortlessly. Dr. Himelhoch's literature review, fitting the "Lines-of-argument (LOA)" model, renders the vital backbone for her arguments conveyed in this mini-monograph. References are used throughout the mini-monograph to further bear out Dr. Himelhoch's work.

With the use of figures, Dr. Himelhoch compiles the data exceptionally well. Her data seems appropriately analyzed and supported by clear language concerning emerging themes. Her interviews produced very rich content, drilled down into ample detail to support Dr. Himelhoch's conclusions. Dr. Himelhoch explains the meaning of the research results and provides an explanation on why these findings are noteworthy. In the discussion section, Dr. Himelhoch takes the opportunity to relate findings to comparable studies. She provides context for other researchers as well as the general public.

Dr. Himelhoch's research is cutting edge and produces a stepping stone to understanding the relationship between exercise and managerial leadership style via quantitative research methods.

Criterion Score: 10 (High): Exceptional

Index

Author's Biography

Carol Himelhoch received her PhD from the University of Michigan. She is professor of management and organizational behavior at Siena Heights University in Adrian, Michigan. Her management experience spans Tier 1 automotive manufacturing operations, marketing, advertising, and retail management. Carol contributes to the field of management by publishing in peer-reviewed journals and speaking at management and leadership conferences. Carol has been active in consulting since the mid 1980s and is co-owner of NeoLogix, LLC (www.neologix-llc.com). She has been an avid HIIT athlete since 2005.

Copy Editor's Biography

Michele Spilberg Hart, MA, is a freelance editor, non-profit director, and yoga teacher. She graduated from the University of Rochester, Rochester, New York, with degrees in Anthropology and Journalism and from Emerson College, Boston, Massachusetts, with a Master of Arts degree in Writing & Publishing.

At Emerson she served as head proofreader of the Beacon Street Review. Following graduation Michele edited several medical journals in the Boston area, was on staff as a copy editor at a Boston area paper, and wrote numerous press releases, reviews, articles, and marketing materials for a variety of publications and corporations. She has more than seven years of experience in corporate marketing communications and 10 years working in the non-profit world.

She is also a registered yoga teacher, completing her 200-hour study with Natasha Rizopoulos, as well as Relax and Renew™ Training with Judith Hanson Lasater, PhD. Michele teaches classes and workshops in the greater Boston area. You can find out more about Michele at www.effortandeaseyoga.com or
www.mshmanagement.com.

Thank you for reading!
We invite you to share your thoughts and reactions

Please write a custom review for this title on:

www.MindBodyMedPress.com

Spring Lake | Michigan | United States

Or simply share the title with your friends via: